Shit My Dad's Dog Says

Lexi 2015

by John Hugh "Daddog" Lewis

Published By
Life By Design Publishing
836B Southampton Road #269, Benicia, CA 94510 U.S.A.
707-751-1665
www.lbdi.us

Cover design by Mark Michael Lewis
Book design by Mark Michael Lewis
Editing Team: Melinda L. Lewis
               Lexi Lewis

Printed in United States

ISBN-10: 0-9743740-5-9
ISBN-13: 978-0-9743740-5-5

This book collects the insights and musings of Lexi-dog Lewis, as interpreted by John Hugh "Daddog" Lewis, in the first year of her life in the Lewis household. It tells the story (in Dog Inglish) of how Lexi comes to claim and rule her domain, winning the hearts of everyone involved.

Through a series of humorous and poignant commentaries on her daily experience, Lexi gives a dog's eye perspective on the life of a retired electrician, his wife (Momdog), friends, and children in their various adventures.

Welcome to the world of Shit My Dad's Dog Says.

December 21, 2014

Hi my name is LEXI DOG.. LEWIS…. notice my blue eyes,, I have very sharpe teeth aad claws… apparently I have already saved my family alot of loot… they were going to get new furniture anf new carpet.. due to my arrival they have put those plans on hold… I am eight weks old…. Mark and Min came over and fell in love we me DUH.. Mark took some pictures of

December 21, 2014

good morning…..I sang pretty much alnight. hoping Momdag would come and visit me.. she did twice… Daddog said if he could sleep thru his kids crying I wasn't a problem… good to see him too… we went outside… something about getting the paper… I like him but sometimes his mind works funny.

December 22, 2014

HA HA HA…I got em… (background) They put me in my crate in their bedroom… to sleep…… I don't think so.. so the laundry room is where I SLEEP… Radio…toys… food water and newspapers (they think I can read)..,,so last night I sang for awhile and sometime in the night or morning I dsicovered a new use for my sharpe claws… I pried the sliding pocket door open and went up stairs to find them .. their sleeping.. Daddog hears something… It's me I'm in my crate eating a bone.. SURPRISE … I await my next test.

December 23, 2014

just got back from my first vet visit….it was Ok.(small K) got new food treats,, and lots of pets… the vet.. a lady.. was over joyed to see such a fine new puppy…. said something about a new house… or car and vacation… I must be very special… said she would like to see me alot…I heard

December 23, 2014

No escape last night… score one for Daddog…. I did fake him out .. He came to get me this morning and thought I had done a HOT& STEAMY ON the floor… fooled him it was my brown mole toy….. I have found some things are better left outside.

December 24, 2014

Spent all day down at Corey's place ..helping MOM and DADdog do some fixing…I learned what a skill saw, nail gun, compressor and two married people sound like…. Momdog mentioned something about a lawyer… didn't catch all of it.. but Daddog did… sounded like we will be doing more stuff together this winter… Daddog said it will be a COLD day…. nice to be home.

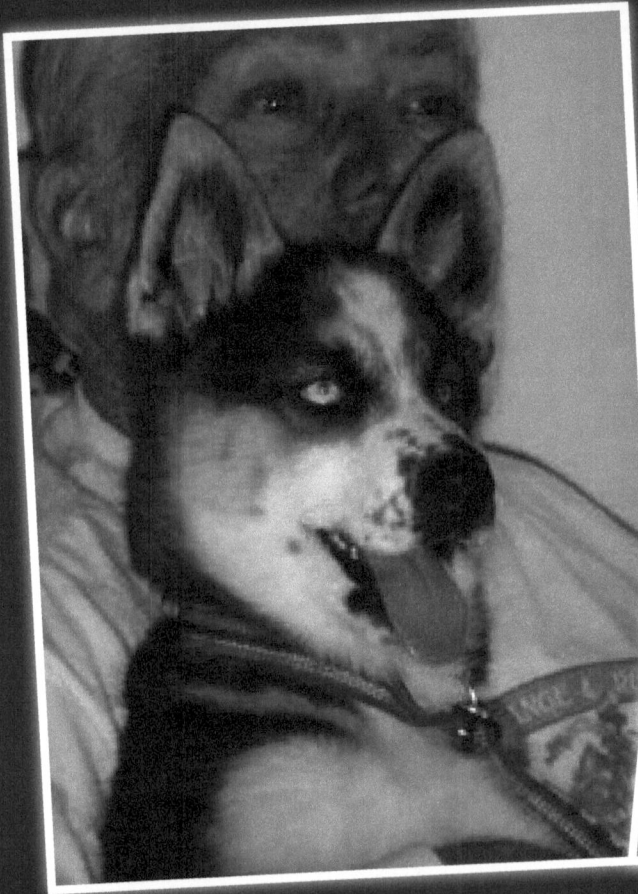

December 24, 2014

December 25, 2014

December 25, 2014

another fine day… dry night … saved it for outside…. Daddog thought it was fantastic,…. we will see how I feel tonight… didn't sing much…. I'm thinkin their bedroom might be in my future… whatever christmas is I wish everybody a great one… I'm told this is my first.

what kind of Dog parents would leave their new puppy home on Christmas eve…. mine….. hope they get a lump of coal from Santa (who ever he/she is)……They said they had a wonderful time seeing all the family and that some of them thought I was cute….SOME….. sounds like a pretty tough family ….hope they come by to meet me soon so I can get all of them onboard. (even if they have Wet hair)… (better be something under that tree)….I feel full of energy tonight… might be along night for them… Merry Christmas.. to all.

I must have the Christmas spirit… I sang every song I knew last night.. (and some I didn't). I'd be quiet for awhile then birst into song….thought maybe someone would come join me..(heard, this morning, they didn't sleep thru it).. well maybe tonight….. we got the paper this morning or as I call it a new piddle spot.. Hope everybody get lots of Stuff.

December 26, 2014

Different Pages:::: I am an early riser.. (always have been)… Momdog and Daddog not so much… they appear to be willing to compromise but are moving in that direction at a slower pace than I had hoped….. being a Crack of dawn girl and taking mutipul naps during the day seems to work for me…as we travel down lifes path together.. (I like that phrase)..(for this early in the morning)..I am confident a mutual starting time be agreed upon…..a special thanks to Santa ? for all the new toys.

December 27, 2014

I'm into Theme songs .. the standards… like my latest.. Ninety Nine Bottles of Beer on the wall..(don't know it ask someone OLD)…. it takes roughly 8 seconds per verse… 99 verses..972 seconds..or 1 hr 40 mintues.. I like to start singing about 3.45 or 4 am…..gets me goin…. Daddog can't get past about 53 verses before he comes to take me outside… sometimes he falls asleep watching T V during the day .. of coarse I am on his lap..WIN…WIN.

December 28, 2014

Played Fetch with Daddog this morning… it was fun…..We are having some disagreements about what things should be Chewed… teeth are for chewin..right? enough said….I see a time when we all look at that chair leg and laugh.. remembering the Cute Days…they don't see it as building memories…. what is compromise.. and why should I.?. got to run … time for Daddog to "get the paper".

December 30, 2014

Daddog is trying to get me to apply less pressure when biteing on huiman flesh… apparently as humans age the skin they've been using doesn't take the kind of beating it used to.. And that's "MY PROBLEM"…rules suck!!

December 30, 2014

4.11…7.25 ….. gettin better….Momdog takes over tomorrow….(Daddog is going huntin)… they call it "emptyin the Dog" works for me… the crate is .mm.. ok…. I am a very trustworthy dog.. told Daddog to leave the door open….. he laughed. ,I get more mature everyday…. where's my dinosaur.?

December 28, 2014

A follow up::: We just went out and got the Paper and he tries to get me to put it in my mouth…. using my teeth.. Is it me… or is that a MIXED message ?

December 29, 2014

Thanks to Daddogs friend John Cochran… I graduated to the big room.. yep slept in the crate all night … didn't feel the need to sing… Daddog got up with me at 3:56 and At 7:03… there will be a nap in his future…. John had suggested a cardboard box along side the bed…. but all Daddog could find was one from a refirgerator…. so the crate is my new sleeping spot … … I have noticed that Daddog sure doesn't say much at 4 am… but he was pleased with the outcome (pun intended).

January 2, 2015   Daddog just got home from hunting… had a good time … showed my picture to his blind partner Rick..(I know I didn't get it either) Rick thought I was a cutie..DUH… another fan…. It will be good to have Daddog home…. I have been sleeping all night…I told Momdog that is why they call it the Crack of Dawn..when I hear that crack I'm ready for piddlin…….Happy New year!!!,……Dogs are lucky ..we get 7 new years a year…. I like Math… I was laying on the couch and realized that every 52nd day i'm a year older.. Momdog said something about the Terrible Two's.. what's that about?

January 3, 2015

I am now being referred to as a She Devil Dog…. Geezers can't hang…I'm a PUPPY get over it… chewing stuff is what I do…on another note my fur is " softer than s baby's butt".. Momdog said It would make a nice coat… she shouldn't have left that sweater where I could get it… sleeping all night… anymore remarks like the"coat" and that could change.

January 4, 2015

Alfie came by to see me….He is my new Dog friend… we have been having a great time…I am alittle bigger than he is but he has a certain presence about him that I like… I had met Rocky from across the street .. but Daddog was holding me so we just touched noses… Alfie plays with me …Rocky was nice.. I can see us being friends.. I am one Lucky girl.

January 4, 2015

Six am wake up call… tried something new .. came back in and went to sleep on Daddogs lap for an hour Daddog was very pleased.. I heard him purring… Alfie isn't up yet.. maybe I wore him out…..Hope he's ready for some fun….eight o'clock

January 4, 2015

I always sleep better when one of my Paws it toughing my family…

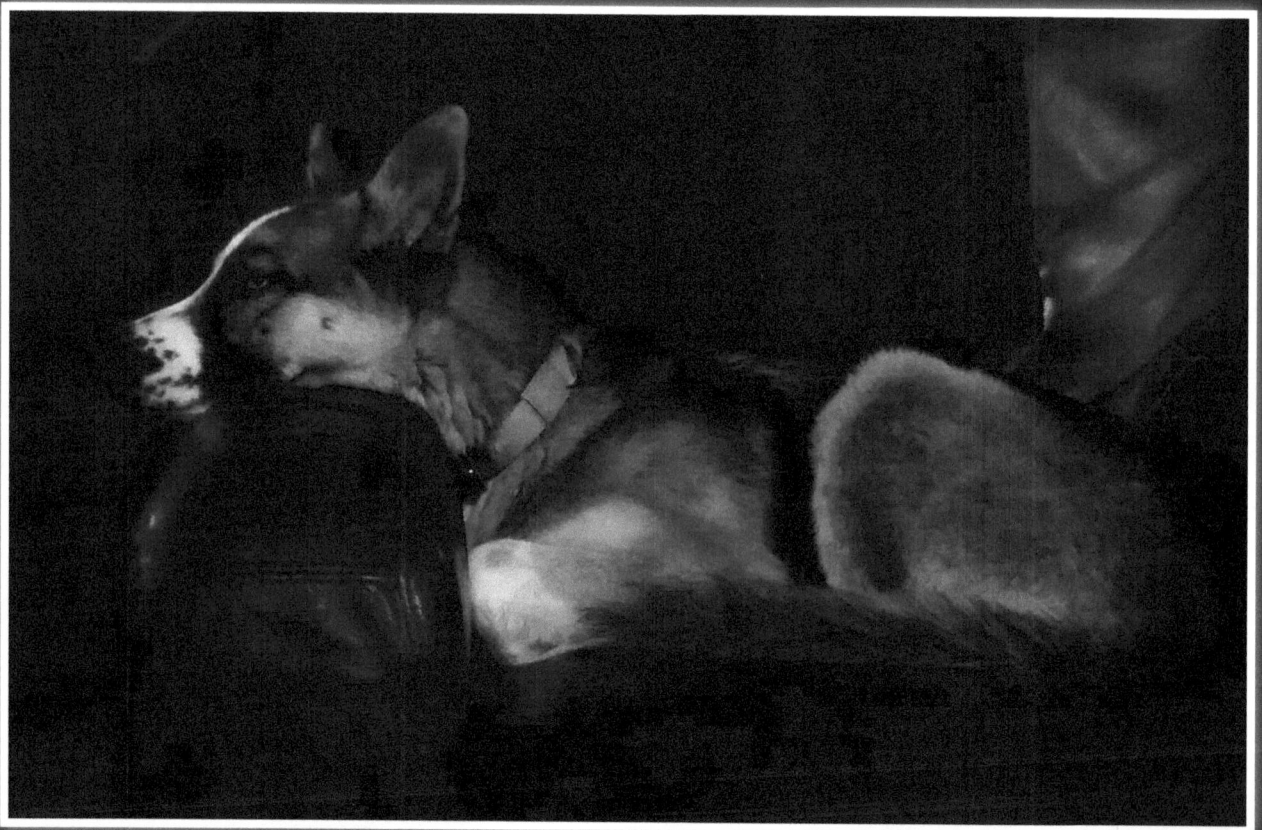

January 5, 2015

I am being called alittle TERD…just because I am hogging all the attention and getting between Alfie and his Mom… Daddog and Alfie are the only guys in this house… Girl are a rulein..I feel the need to ignore everything Daddog says.. like the other females do… it might come back to haunt me .. but I'll deal with that later …it's good to be the Queen.

January 5, 2015

Early morning….. Daddog got up to "check" something in the bathroom.. at 3.07…. Play time…..The Moon was really bright…He thought I should go back to sleep after our walk…. Hey I'm awake now… I let the "House" know I wasn't havin anymore of that create.. (due to his concern for others) WE went downstairs to sleep on the couch..Daddog takes up alot of room on the couch..but we (I) fell back to sleep.. Daddog didn't purr that much…..probably had things on his mind… I tried to convey the bonding thing… he can be alittle dense.

January 6, 2015

Did anyone hear those Trumpets blownin…. to celebrate my first night out of the crate… funny story… the scene…. Bed time around the old Lewis household… the crate is opened.. I'm placed in "MY" crate.. for 15 minutes I plea my case..suddenly Daddog as a vison… me on my leash (gripped tightly in his hand) lyin QUIETLY …beside the bed… Trumpets sound fade to Darkness…. Score 1 for Lexi Dog.

January 7, 2015

TO WHOM IT MAY CONCERN……. I usaully sit on Daddogs lap while I dictate my thoughts to him.. occasionally I ask him to misspell some words to make it real… Daddog graduated from Wasamatteryou.. with Bullwinkle…………………………(did they buy it?).

January 7, 2015   I'm confused…. why do Humans … sit on my water bowl,?

January 8, 2015

Bernie Morrison is full of Do Do..He told Daddog … it is not necessary to (when giving a treat) to give a big piece of the treat.as long as you give THEM something…. that is Horse Shit… I LOVE Duck breasts from costco…. I saw Daddog cutting them up with sissors… …He is gonna pay…I may just unfriend his ass.

January 8, 2015

We are shopping for a Real bed for me….I spied a very nice one that will fit my needs perfctly… It's a California King and guess what ..it's already in the Bedroom…. What is a Vote and why do I only get one?… They seem to make alot of decisions FOR me… I know thier heart is in the right place…. But.

January 13, 2015

I thought someone was playing a joke on me…. I like to squeeze between the wall and the recliner.. lately it has been getting alittle tight… thought they had pushed the chair closer to the wall… Well I went to the vet today…..sat. on the scale and found that I am a 21 pounder girl… this also explains why Momdog was huffin and puffin when she carried me downstairs….. I discovered some common mistakes that people make when taking a stool sample to the vet…. how much is to much and it doesn't have to be warm.

Shit My Dad's Dog Says - John Hugh Lewis

January 13, 2015

I don't know what my options were......
but I think I did O K....Momdog and
Daddog maybe difficult at times but
they seems trainable.. who says cute can
only take one so far...I do this thing
with my eyes that even had the vet
asking permisson to take my photo for
her Facebook page... of coarse I went
along... maybe I need an agent... The vet
kept going on and on about what a cutie
I was...Momdog finally ask her to stop...
(. apparently she charges by the hour).....
Party pooper. .

January 13, 2015

I have observed...Mom and
Daddog ask each-other the same
question alot....What.?....I know
their ears are small but......I have
always been a Talker.. I hardly ever
say What... Maybe it's because
their ears are so far apart..... poor
design.

January 14, 2015

Had my first therapy session today...
just kiddin... I have all the answers (to
all of the questions that concen me)...It's
simple... look cute and pretend to obey
their comands. Pee and Poo outside.. don't
chew cowboy boots or leather purses... in
the early morning hours wait for the human
d'jour to pidddle before I do.....I'm told I
got it made.. that's a matter of opinion..
Therapy yeah right.

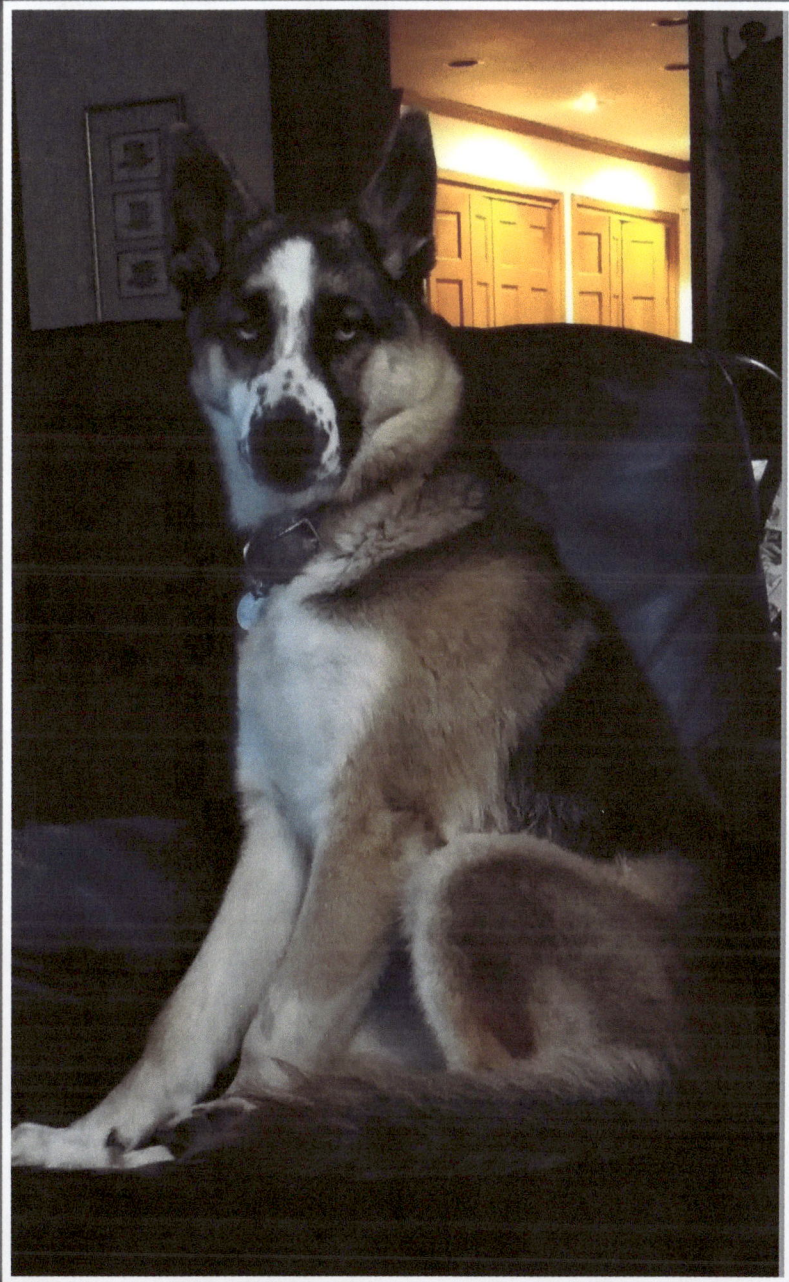

January 14, 2015

Always willing to grow and experience new things... I was offered and
excepted the chance to try. KFC broiled. chicken skin... Yummy... I give
it two Paws up..(the meat ain't to shabby either)... the Duck Momdog
cooked last night is also on my favorite list....Daddog was cleaning some
Ducks and gave me a sniff...Oh yeah.. sat right under Momdog while she
was prepareng them... ... I'm trying to picture myself as a Duck dog... I
figure if you don't think outside the crate.... why be here.

January 19, 2015

Daddogs home…. to celebrate we all went for a ride in the truck…I destoryed it… ….Back ground…. everytime I ride in a motor vehicle ..I empty my tummy.. the vet says it has something to do with my inner ear… Doctor Morrison (yes.. Bernie) says you need to keep going for rides "she'll out grow it"… don't ask how that working for Daddog…… back to the present…Daddog put down plastic and towels to CATCH the mess… luckly I found a gap….he had a gun case and a huntin vest.. so I thought why mess up a perfectly good towel.. to add a new wrinkle I used both of my ends…..Let's just say Daddog is glad he's home.

January 20, 2015

Something is going down … I'm not to sure I approve…… This is MY house….so you can imagine my reaction to the news .. we are getting a new member of the family… now I'm still young and don't know everything.(I know that's hard to believe)…. So I ask… what is a White Elephant.. why do we need one… where is it going to sleep… does it have it's own toys… does it think it's going to be a LAP Elephant.. who gets walked first… How much do they cost (fixed income). Has this Elephant been marked down and why.. well stay tuned, Momdog should be home from the White Elephant sale

January 15, 2015

To chew or not to chew….Duh… chew… friction has occured with my choices lately… the puppy excuse is running thin… ..even cute may have reached its limit… chew toys… boring… I do love their squeek…..Hey I'm an easy goin girl…….its call an Antique. because it's OLD… (like OLD, out dated … not made anymore ..and very tastey… am I wrong?

January 16, 2015

I'm alitle pissed … Thought this was going to be my first Duck Hunting trip….apparently there is more to it than showing up with the right attitude…….. something about loud noises… sitting still for long periods… and beleive it or not ..not eating the Ducks… maybe I dodged a Bullet..(pun intended)..It's a good thing I asked… I think I'm to young to hold a grudge….. what ever those are……… now where did I see those Lizard skin cowboy boots.

January 21, 2015　　　Jokes on me.. although I feel I had some concerns that were valid....Momdog had a great time, bought Daddog and Coreydog some neat stuff... (apparently what Daddog wants and what Momdog thinks he'll like are not the same)...He put the things in the Never wear pile...(look out Darin your Birthdays comeing up) ..smiled and said thank you.. ....Can't exchange it.. not even for store credit.... anybody need a LARGE chew toy in the shape of a peanut... The sales girl said it is what you get an Elephant`... I was ...MISS .. lead.

January 21, 2015

I have discovered a new source of chew toys...There are these soft rolls of paper that can be shredded..(. located in an open cloest.) there is even one on the wall by my water bowl..... of coarse shreddin is best done in the dark while they're sleeping... hours of fun... they said it looked like Snow .. and of coarse we get to play Keep-a-way... a new dawn.

January 22, 2015

I think you measure a Dog from tip to tip... ...but the other day at the vet, I saw a dog what...(not that)... had his tail cut down..... life is confusing. and why do some Dogs have short legs ?....there should be a mold?.....To much time in the kitchen by myself... My mind tends to wander.... when do get my own remote?... they're home.... yeah I know... Don't Jump...Don't Jump.. sometimes I think I'm more glad to see them than they are... ahh tummy rub... all is foirgiven.

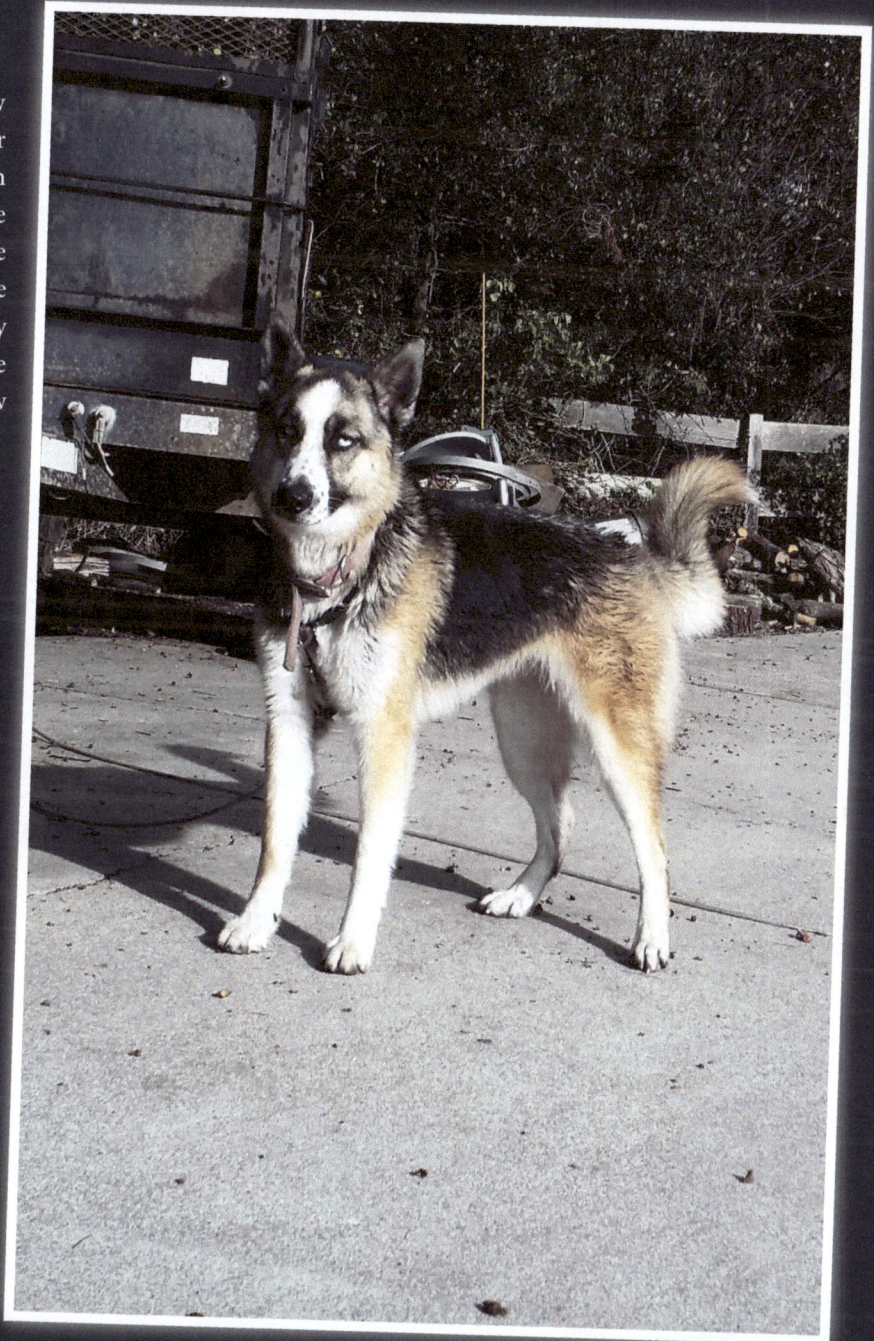

We played a new game….the scene.. Momdog and I are on a walk..(up by the Red truck).. Daddogs is Huntin… Momdog falls on the ground… she pretents like she can't get up… I got to help her drag herself into the house… I bit at her hair and she pretended to swat me away..we had a great romp..She couldn't reach the phone..I jumped up to help her just as CoreyDog happen to call… Corey call some numbers and I got to meet some Firemen and Ambulance people.. they took Momdog away.. It was a great game… I found out it"s called… Relocate or Dislocate your Hip … I don't think we will play it again… Momdog is fine.. Corey stayed with me till she got home.. Daddog drove Home to see her.. never a dull moment around here.

Daddog is home from gettting his Decoys……got to go to Coreydogs house last night… boreing…If the truth be know I prefer to be takein Potty by Daddog…It's like we are a team…Momdog holds a pretty good leash … but… Momdogs Hip.. everybody knows that… O K her wearin around Hip … is appreantly Ok… went to the Doc today and he said as long as she doesn't breath and walk at the same time.. It shouldn't happen again… I think she got this Doc on sale… there goes those dance classes… (I guess some people still have Wet Hair).

I have observed…. The ta-do list might be better referred to as ..Things you better do before you die by accident list….. ..(jury of Wives.. justifiable Homicide)…. Momdog apparently does not like trees… (paper)….that list is looong.. It really doesn't help that Daddog says ..What list?…….. Hey I heard it's time to hunt ..Pheasants.

January 28, 2015

I am a luckydog…. I have speed..where as Momdog.. (hip) Daddog.(old) are no match for the Lexmeister…. every now and then I slip my bonds and go for a run up the hill… I hide behind a bush and listen to them call me…..they try everything…. even brought out my squeek toy… finally I come back …. Win..Win…. of coarse I don't get a treat…… but man it's fun…..who ever said.." have your KIDS when you are young" should have said "don't get a Puppy if you can't hang.

January 29, 2015

I'm a Bowl half full kind of girl…No mater what life throws at me I know it will always get better…so when I saw a new package of Bacon strips…. in the shopping bag .. I was sure they were for me…When some stips were placed in the microwave.. I was confused.. then these same strips were consumed by..OTHERS…I don't need a bunch of excuses..where's mine?… Being the center of the universe is supposed to have certain Perks…. their training shall continue.. No More MISS Nice DOG.

January 28, 2015

Overheard.. Hon… why don't you write that ta-do list on a roll of toilet paper.. so It can I an get some use from it too..?….(didn't go over well) some things are better thought than said outloud.

January 29, 2015

What… they're little people right.. so they sit in antique rocking chairs an have fancy old clothes ..their bodies are hard like some kind of clay or porcelin.. their faces are painted… and they have the most delicious HAIR..I just can't help myself.. Yum Yum… for some reason they have been removed to a Safe location.. Bummer… they are now all Blad…I'm playing the Puppy Card.. Momdog is very upset.. I may be grounded.. in real dirt… I mentioned my freckles … she didn't smile.

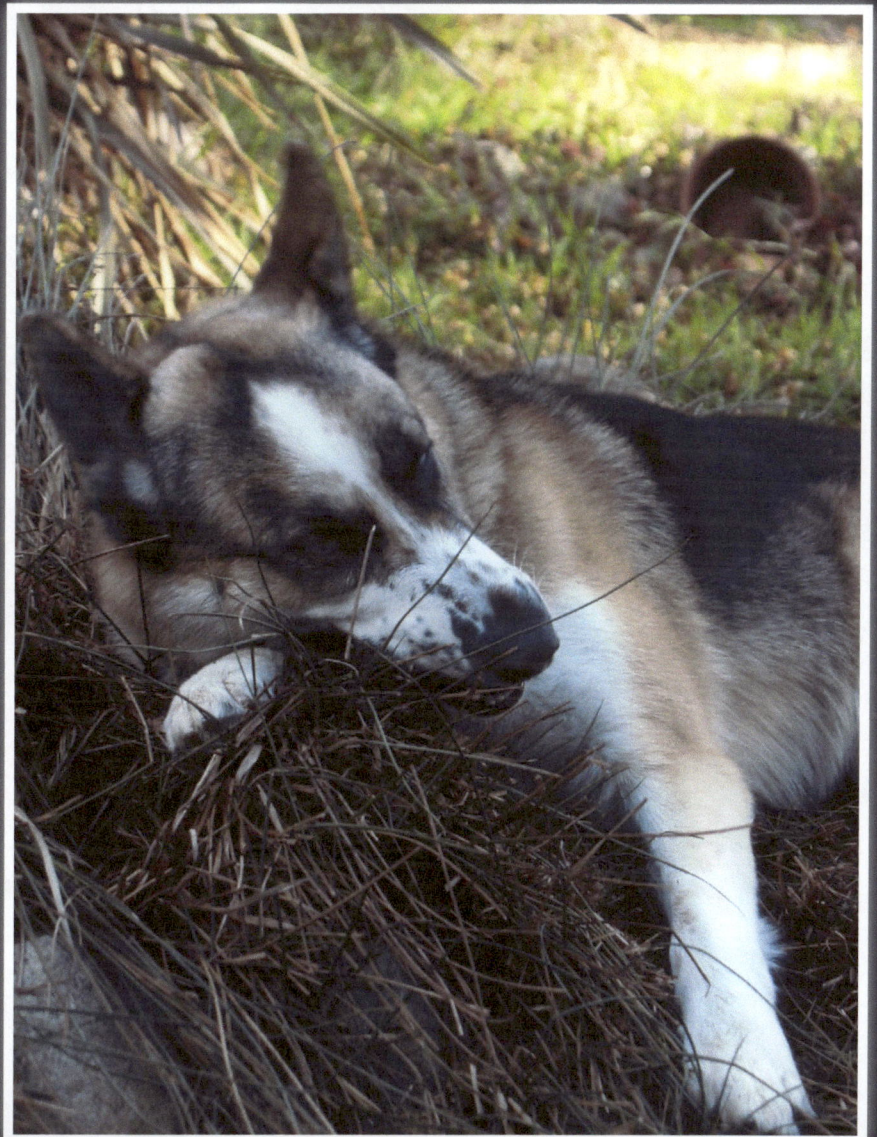

January 30, 2015

What a day Aunt Tyla and Neice Inga came by to see Me…Two more fans added to the club… said they don't believe I could possibly do the things I am accused of…..especially the Dolls Hair.. they said some very nice things about Me… All true of coarse….They brought some dinner for us..(?).. It was delicious. (I'm Told).. they woofed it…. I didn't even get to lick the bowl… I got a new Rope toy.. thank you thank you…Inga took my picture…I tried to hold still …but… I am an active Girl..

January 30, 2015

Is there such a thing as Dog-Nip… If there isn't… I discovered it in… Rawhide chew sticks… I love those suckers.. of coarse around here they are called Furniture savers……… Had an Idea …. Keyboards with the Letters far apart for typing Dogs… You would understand if you had Paws…. Yes I was thinkin of cutting out the Middleman…. don't tell him… he thinks he's special.

January 31, 2015

If your keeping score ..it's Lexi 1 stuffed white rabbit.. 0..Momdog sewed it up a few times,,, now it's just the body of a rabbit.. its head didn't make it….. it does still have some chewin left… maybe it will make a come back..whata way to start a day… where did he put those cowboy boots?

February 1, 2015

to whom it may concern….. The King James bible in miniture form.. that used to be on display in the entry area….. valued at … lets just say … any people that stand to inherit.. anything from the Lewis estate. should adjust their outlook… I found it very good (reading) chewing .. to say it is nolonger in pristine condition would be accurate… On a side note .. turning those little pages with my paws was very difficult … I found using my teeth and tonuge worked much better… for a first addition you would think they would have used bigger paper.. however the leather cover was delicious.

February 1, 2015

I went to the Dog park… didn't see one Dog parked..(Bad I know,, stay with me). Met some other Dogs.. they could tell it was my first time… I hid under a chair Momdog was sitting in.. not proud of it but shit happens…. I finally started to run around.. but I sure liked that chair…I feel good about the experience… and willing to go again….. in other news… it was just a Bible.. from what I hear every hotel room has one and those are full size and free.

February 2, 2015

Monday....Got up early ready to go.. had to drag Daddog out of bed...He apparently counts the early morning walks as haveing been up already....On the agenda today .. chewin.. .. never gets old... found a piece of sprinkler pipe... buried.... had alittle trouble getting it free.... many twists and fittings fits perfect in my mouth and makes a really good crunching sound... they are supposed to be cutting back on using water anyway ....I'm Helping.

February 3, 2015

I'm a CHEWER... not to say I'm proud of it... it's just what I do... today ichewed my call–er in 2.. Momdog fixed it....(why).

February 3, 2015

Apparently.. The Wee..(get it).... hour trips in the morning are due to...Well we went to the vet and she told us to limit the amount of liquids that are consumed after 9 pm.... Now both Momdog and I have to really watch to see that Daddog doesn't drink beyond that hour...everybody wins

February 4, 2015

Well we did the usaul early morning trip .. good outcome... Daddog had a meetin..which ment 6 am get up.. we arrived back at our asigned sleeping places at 4.26.. I have noticed.... sometimes Daddog has trouble gettong back in snooze mode... I thought a renade might help>>>not the singing kind ..the crunching kind..I chewed on my Pvc coupling for alittle over an hour.. didn't even get a pet.. I guess it's the thought that counts.

February 5, 2015

I've got the title..... 50 shades of brown. or leaving my mark.. it's the story of Momdog trying to match the color of the table leg I chewed..... another of my literary works ... Hey I think that is going to leave a stain... still in the works.... It's asks the question .. why are rugs so absorbent.. and... Liquids shouldn't they all be clear....What did you think I did all day..?. welcome to my world.

again today.... can't wait to see her treasures..... my favorites of coarse have to do with Hero Dogs..usually Huskie Shepard Mix. or Dogs in commercials... or Puppies that are to cute for words...(hearing stories of my you't.)(cousin Vinney.) never fails to bring a smile...to both our faces... or maybe he'll fix some Bacon... just heard some great news ... Bernie and Daddog are buying a Toyhauler..... Hey I'm getting more toys...Yeah.

sometimes I feel they have forgoten why they are in my life........ I am told the saying goes something like this.....It does not gather food... it does not serve Vaul... but it does seem pleaseing to them... What else could it be...... Petting a Puppy ... (note to daddog ..keep it recent).

supposed to take cooky dough off the baking trays on the counter..... very tasty..(yeah I know BAD DOG) on a positive note my vertical reach....... (standing on my Hind legs) is really improving... Hey i can get that for you....... hope those cookies are done soon... Momdog make a really good cooky.

Shit My Dad's Dog Says - John Hugh Lewis

February 9, 2015

February 9, 2015

February 11, 2015

self absorbed… I don't think so… I sneak in and read many posting on face book…. With that said… Uncle Mark posts some profound shit.. thought provoking, emontioally challenging almost forcing "one" to look inside ones self… (chip) (as in off the old block)… So naturally it occured to me that when I am told to "GET DOWN".. is my creativeness being stiffled by the MAN… and will this effect how I am viewed by the World…Next time I see uncle Mark… extra kisses.

You decide….Daddog left his wallet in a pair of pants ,,, Momdog washed them..("I don't check pockets") (Momdogs Mantra)… Items were removed …..wallet left to dry….. Well it was where it was left to dry that envolves me… You guessed it … near the edge of the counter….NEWS FLASH… Momdog just came to my defense… seems she had retrived an old wallet that was exactly the same style and color as the wet one… and THAT one was the one I chewed up…. so I only destroyed a non-used item.. Daddog loves me again…. I do love the taste of leather…I wear a coat …if you wear pants …empty the pockets.

Went to the vet… sat on the scale… 28.3 lubs (lbs) at that rate I will weigh 84lubs when I am a year old,, looking forward to being an all grown up.Dog….. Daddog says Growning Up isn't all it's cracked up to be… said he wouldn't wish it on anybody….. He says getting older is ok, but growing up is a Bit*h… I think this constitutes Raining on my Parade…….Valentines Day is comeing..saw Momdog looking for Last years Card for Daddog..(.of coarse he saved it) (it's 20 years old). she says she feels the same so why buy a new card…such a Romantic…..

February 12, 2015

I am assured the action about to be described will result in no disruption of POSTS..... The scene... I am lying on the kitchen floor.. Daddog questions "what's in your mouth?" nothin I respond... NUTTIN-A (blazeing Saddles REF) a chase ensues and I am bribed to Open my Mouth... where upon the Plastic bottom of Daddogs Mouse drops from My mouth.. what ever happened to...No harm No foul... Hey the Mouse still works... this is the kind of crap I have to endure.

February 13, 2015

I feel bad for Momdog... she wants ACTION(control) so bad.. and Daddog is OUT OF IT ... she'll ask" so when are you going to do———-".. the answer is always the same... ".soon" that DADDOG is a slippery devil......In other news...my formal education is being put on hold.. heard I won't get TUTORED until I'm 6 to 8 months old... they can be so confusing.

February 11, 2015

Markdog...(upgraded status) took my photo while he was talking to Daddog on Skype....I feel I have a reasonable expectation of privacy and that my Dog Rights have been violated...However... rather than consult a Dog attorney... (due the many positive coments about said photo) ..I . have..decided. to just say Thanks................................ from what I understand prints can be ordered on line.......(just a thought).

February 13, 2015

We all live in the same structure… so why would Daddog be in a Doghouse….Momdog says he's an Under-achiver ..only 2 chores were completed yesterday… so she added 3 more…. she runs a tight ship…Daddogs says he wishes he was like me… everything I do is PRECIOUS… it's good to be the Queen.

February 14, 2015

I'm a Smart Dog…I know what Love is (Forest GumpISH) Hearing all the Wonderful stories of True everlasting Love.. How Having found that one special one makes your life complete.. How having that wonderful someone to walk thru life with is the greatest feeling in the world.. the closeness, the warm feeling just hearing their name the tear that comes when you realize just how lucky you are …. with that said ….FOR A GOOD TIME CALL…LEXI…867-5309.

February 16, 2015

Got a baff today….not my favorite thing ..but atleast they used warm water….. over heard….Size matters….what size Tv will fit in the new Toyhauler… Daddogs says …with the condition of his Eyes ..the bigger the better… Momdog thinks (……….)..(. its a good thing she doesn't read this stuff). that an Existing T V would be just fine… Daddogs thinkin 60☒ Momdogs thinkin 6☒,,, The god news is there is something called Morrison Bucs… 2 against 1…. I'm thinkin 2 remotes..

February 20, 2015

Bernie thinks I might have PAW-TEN-SHAUL… Had a Great time with my new DOM-In-ate-Trix friend SKY… to say I was schooled in proper behavior would be an under statement… SKY has things she wants done a certain way and that's the way they are done,,, she had appatently not heard I was the Queen…. I look forward to her next visit… can't say I will improve… it's fun messing with her………. I learned SKY has a limit.

February 16, 2015

I slept great… Momdog not so much, something to do with "what if the list gets lost"… and Will Dadogs health last long enough to finish it….and will she have to DATE again…. and after all, everything on the list is priority one… I think shes like." Trying to PUSH a CHAIN….. of coarse if anyone can… Momdogs the one… (the Dating thing really has her concerned… she has invested alot of time trying to Train Daddog ..but…. possibly a younger model).

February 19, 2015

I had heard many stories about the GREAT an Powerful BERNIE. M.. well From my first impression I'd say they were all true… Bernie brought my new friend SKY Dog down to go Pheasant Hunting with Daddog…Dadddog says SKY is the Best at Pheasant Hunting… They got 5… Sky's ass is Dragin… she said she had forgotten how much fun it was…I can't wait to play with her as soon as she wakes up from her nap… LEXI… Pheasant Dog……. a girl can Dream.

February 21, 2015

Well Daddog just burned up a Pot says it's my fault I took to long to dictate my thoughts… The King of Spin… He's in deep Do Do and he knows it… so he messes up and I get no lunch… Hey Daddog want to go for another Ride?

February 21, 2015

They feel the need to take me for rides in the truck (thanks but the car is no better) Daddog has spread an elaborate mixture of towels and tarps to capture any type of MASS that I may feel like bringing forth…I am proud of him ..so far he batting about 700.. (baseball ref.). the 300 is where I excel….We had to stop at 2 different trash cans to rid the back seat of treasure. I was brought back Home.(Momdog forgot her White Elephant ID) and placed in the garage.. had my Bed ,toys ,water I was empty.. safe in the garage… Remember I said I was very good at opening doors… well the garage (man door) door into the house.. has a handle that is easy. and the door opens in..so. when Daddog returned from taking Momdog, I was in the kitchen.. munching on my plumbing pipe.. I'm pretty sure the sound he made was a laugh.. he called me a Weasel… only thing that saves my butt is …Momdog thinks I'm cute.

February 22, 2015

Good news ….SKY's coming back today…I suppose I should say I'm gonna try to be a better host…. Nah….I think maybe she was just alittle tired…I always say Play While You Can…(A Morrison-ism)…. He is full of .em,,… (note to self… don't jump on Bernies New Truck). .. ……

February 24, 2015

Sky is the BEST….. where as I am doing my best to own the name Weasel.Dog….. (let your mind wander)….Sky is very good natured about all of it… but sometimes she pins me and explains things to me…she can only take having her face licked for so long before all hell breaks loose.. I wear her out..she is really greatful when Bernie says lets go to the barn… sure wish I could go hunting with her…I don't think she feels the same… sometimes I think she considers me as Punishment for something she must have done …. it couldn't have been THAT bad…

February 24, 2015

I watch… I learn… Humans walk on only 2 legs… I have found … standing on my hind legs gives me an opportunity to see what is on the counters…. all kinds of good stuff…apparently this is frowned upon by the High comand.. always willing to experience new things ,I find this is stifling my inquisitive nature , I am trying not to learn the word OFF… Who do I see for Justice…..Sky says.."sometimes lifes a bitch"….I say" there's a new Sheriff in town."

February 26, 2015

Well the early start that was supposed to happen …didn't… B M (Bernie Morrison) (hey that fits) Decided not to beat the traffic and sleep in..problem is I havn't seen my budddy SKY yet… thought we could spend some time together before she left for the mountains… Daddog made Bacon for the occasion… Yum.. there is always a bright side.

February 26, 2015

Did I ever mention that I Love DADDOG….there are many reasons.. which I won't bother to go into now…. lets just say three words….. COSTCO CHICKEN SKIN….. it seems there is a family tradition..that when returning from Costco The Dog dejuer ..Me… gets the skin from a….. I-say I-say .a ROASTEN CHICKEN…Heh Heh Heh……that's some. good eatin son….No.. I don't beliieve LOVE is skin deep ..but it's a start.

February 27, 2015

I don't cook… I eat…. that being said… how would you Freezer Burn something… and wouldn't that be an OXYMORON ? This world gets more confusing all the time… and why would anyone belittle an Ox… Humans can be so shallow.

February 28, 2015   Why would..D O G or is it G O D give me the abilkity to stand on my hind legs and reach the counters of this world.. if I wasn't supposed to.. I feel if I don't use the gifts i am given.. I will be considered an under achiver.not being an achiver (or is it retriever) is what being a Dog is all about (Which is considered a sin in the Dog world) and would someone please tell me what are lines and why do they need to be Drawn. and should they apply to me. if I knew there were so many rules I would never have leaned how to read............ for those who are keeping score... it's Lexi 1 dinosaur 0 In fact I think I swalloed its squeeker... Daddog said he would watch my stools... I don't even sit on stools.

February 28, 2015

Lying here on the floor .with my back touching Daddogs foot… life is Good … Dadog thinks he's the lucky one… I know better.

March 1, 2015

went for another ride today…...no out come…. but I drooled more than was in my body.. I know, but I did it.. in other news I think a nap is in my future.. Momdog says Markdog might be able to hip-mo-tize me..something about stareing at a swinging Dog bone and not eating it.. and counting backwards… and I don't even count forwards that well… yeah that's my cup of tea..so far WE have tried .. the chewables.. dram-ma meen.. and ben a drill.. today WE tried tuffing it out…. I really wish WE could get a handle on this…... I hear the call of far away places… faint but it's there.

March 4, 2015

Daddog just got home from a Lions breakfast meeting…. unharmed…. to make him feel special I acted like I hadn't seen him in a year… jumping, kisses, biting, the whole thing… he ate it up…I can be very affectionate.. speaking of CATS… those darn (cleaned up for our younger readers) Cats were back … I grabbed Daddogs hand and tried to get him to open the back door. so I could explain the need for their Departure..He didn't get it.. once again very dense..(I try, but I don't think there is Hope for him)… I even used small words… feel my frustration… a DOGS life… I've tried spelling it out for him… but as you know I don't spell that well… maybe he'll read what he's writing…. yeah right.

March 2, 2015

Sky seems very happy… I think it's because she's going home… Daddog said she was great today..(extra great) so all the birds on their card are shot… I am really going to miss Sky.. I will have to go back to bugging my humans… I heard some talk about maybe us taking a trip to a place called Tahoe.. it is supposed to be near Skys house .. Sky doesn't seem to be as excited as I am …. I might have been to puppyish..(is that possible?)

March 4, 2015

t's not like I'm havin a great day…. first Sky left this mornng.. I thought I was a pretty good host… got a "have your people call my people" look from her..as she drove away…maybe my feelings are hurt.or maybe I just miss her…. then… 2 CATS were in my yard this evening…I'd seen them in the neighbors yard but not mine… I was inside.. they come walkin thru my back yard like they owned it.. I gave them my best "get the ___ out of my yard bark.. they ignored me… ignored ME… next time that happens I'm going thru the screen….would have tonight but the door was closed… some people lke CATS… this is a DOG house.. when I get my fenced in yard we'll see just how fast they are… they won't be ignoring ME.

March 5, 2015

I am beside myself….Let me ask ..how would you feel if you found another Dog in your house… not just another Dog.. but a Dog that looks just like you….well it happened… I'm sitting watching T V with my Humans.. when I look over to the left of the T V and guess what I see…. there inside the glass door of the Stero cabinet is another Dog.. at first it scared the crap out of me… then I started to get mad… seeing this other Dog in my house explains alot… food missing ,toys not where I left them, Dog hair where I couldn't have possibly been.. THEY say I'm imagining things… but everytime I look in that cabinet.. the Dog is there..I'm not going to take this kind of disrespect, it's either Me or Her..(it's a girl Dog I can tell)..I know I should be the bigger Dog and offer a (olive) bone(branch) but I feel it's Her move……either she goes or I do…………………….. more later.

March 7, 2015

Heard a noise downstairs last night….. this morning my toys were all over the place.. there was a half eaten chew stick near the T V… ater bowl empty, food almost gone.. Momdogs says "they were like that" when we went up to bed … I know better… I checked the cabinet and She's still in there… they won't even look… What has to happen before they believe me?.. I think She has been inviting those CATS into the back yard…..I am going to sneak down-stairs and catch Her in the act… I don't know anything about cameras…I don't think my paws can work the buttons… but I've got to do something.. wish me luck.

March 8, 2015

Rober suggested I set a trap for the girl in the cabinet….Isa would say capture the moment… I decided to do both…I went to the cabinet looked right at Her… put my nose against the glass..she did the same.. now all we have to do is open the door and Her nose print will be the evidence I need… I not only have Her nose print I found out Her name it's IXEL.. said so right on Her collar…. the pieces are falling into place.

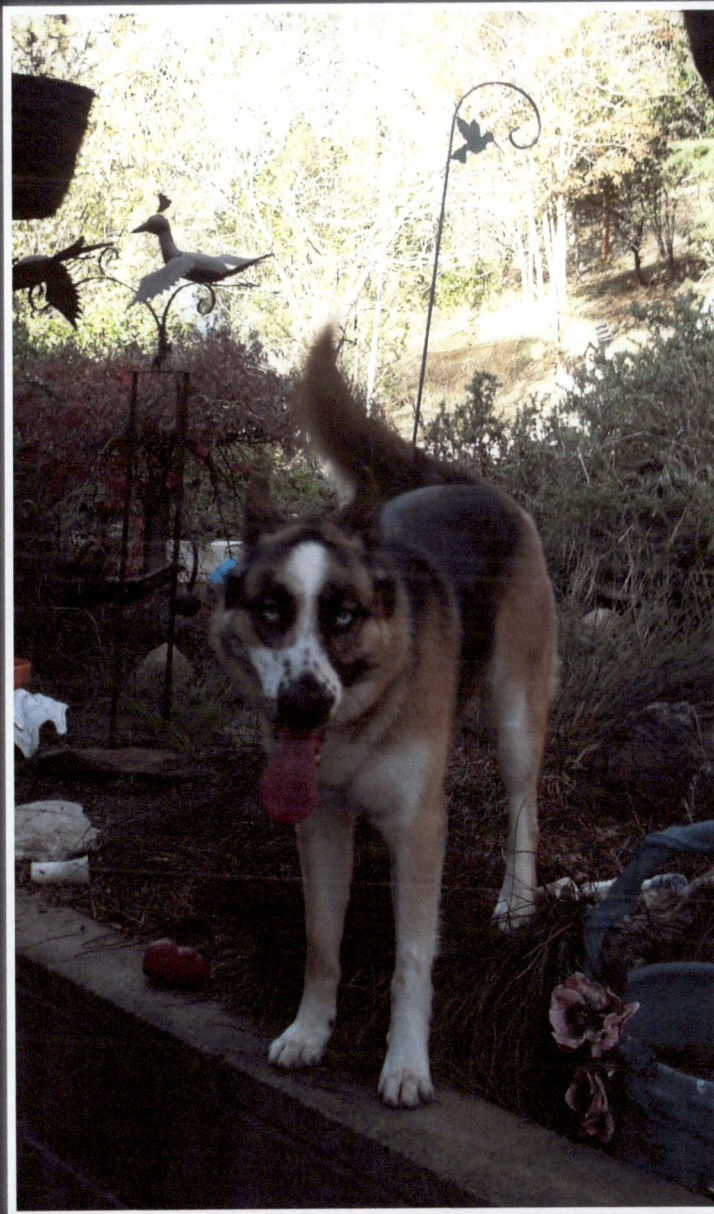

March 9, 2015

Liitle known fact;; TODAY IS FORGIVE YOUR PET FOR CHEWING UP YOUR GOOD STUFF...DAY

Shit My Dad's Dog Says - John Hugh Lewis

March 9, 2015

Monday... someone messed with the clocks... Forgive your Dog day was a big sucess.. It seems some places celebrate it quite often (A Z ref) (LISA Daddog says he feels your pain) I hope It catches on in this area..... the conspiracy continues... maybe it will be made into a series... Hey I could be the Star... Daddog got me some new food and treats some place call PET.. something ...Dropped Dana's name.. had to listen to 2 hrs of how wonderful she is.........got a rewards card.....got to go... Momdag got a leather jacket for Daddog at the Elephant sale.... if it's to big for the Elephant how's Daddog supposed to wear it? It looks YUMMY

March 10, 2015

Rambleings When Channeling it is wise to pick someone who is... well whoes mind is not all cluttered with .. lets just call them Smarts... .. I have definetely choosen well...... It is with a heavy heart that I fear I might have caused some damage to this receptor... But sometimes Sh*t happens....and this is the only Horse I got..... is that wrong?

March 11, 2015

I made friends with IXEL.. we set some boundries .. I even gave her permission to play with some of my toys.(the ones without squeekers ofcoarse)..She is only allowed to come out after my bedtime...I hope she doesn't realize how beautiful she is ... that could be a problem... we'll see how it goes

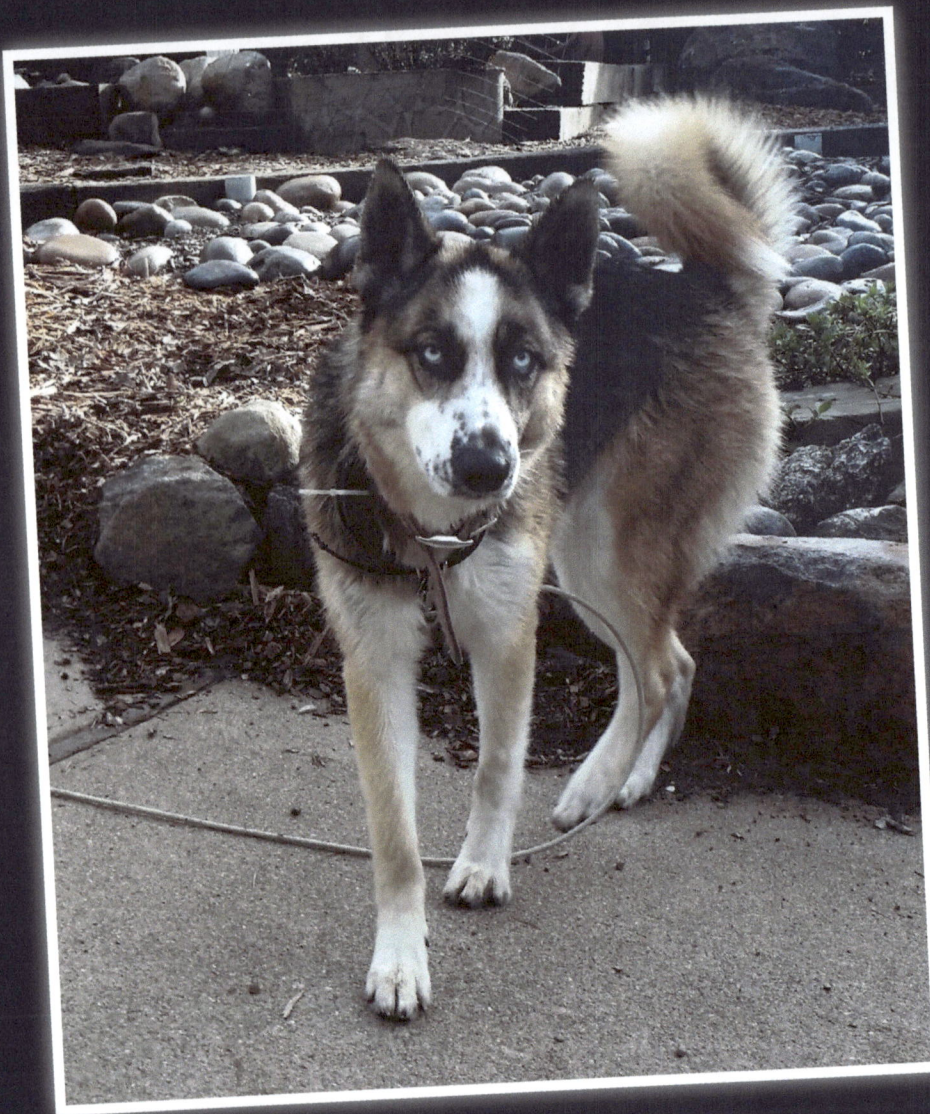

March 15, 2015

Daddog showed me a picture of the Panama canal from space...there was a tattoo of wreath right below it... upon closer examination it was Bernies scar from his surgery.... I think his days of wearin a full body swimsuit have begun... don't want to scare the litttle children out of the water.. Best wishes for a quick recovery... BERNIEDOG

March 16, 2015

I was told not to RUN in the house... I felt they were being very .... Well I wasn't careful.. my front right leg hit the edge of the cedar chest.....hope it's just a bruise..10 am appt;,...the good news is they have treats at the vet... always a silver lining.............................I probably shouldn't have gone for the sympathy thing.

March 16, 2015

Back from the Vet... just a bruise.. got a treat.. threw up in the back seat..... (Daddog was prepared). another day in the life of the LEXIMIESTER...we all had a good laugh when the doctor said I should lead a Quite life for a week.

March 12, 2015 ·

Ya see that dark clould...........There might be a burial in our future... My stuffed Rabbit... only pieces remain.. still some good chewin on the arms and legs but I fear his days are coming to an end........ of coarse it will be a closed shoebox..(.actually a matchbox will probably be fine)... for a Rabbit with no squeeker (never had one) he has lasted a long time. and served his purpose...... I guess it's almost time to remember the good times and move on... Iguess they don't makem like the used to,...., but then again how would I know......... anyone have a matchbox?

March 13, 2015

SKY sent me a tell-a path-ick message that OLD BernieDog (UPGRADE).. was having a Tummy tuck...She said from what she hears...(they won't let her Visit) BernieDog is doing pretty good... seems to really have gottin the Bed Pan thing Down......... Daddog said he has a plan to sneek a BM into the hospital so His Buddy can go home... I said ..he is a BM.

March 17, 2015

So Old Berniedog is hangin in there... in alot of pain.. I offered to send up one of my best chew sticks ..for him to bite on... Ok so I might have broken it in alittle.. but it's got some good chewin left in it.... Hey.. I'm here for him..... I'm so happy he liked my PINK flowers...Hey PINK is the New Brown.... speaking of Brown.... the offer still stands.

March 17, 2015

This Ride stuff is kickin my butt... Question is how much can the backseat of the truck hold.... trip to Tahoe should be a tummy emptying experence..... on a brighter note.... I almost caught a Turkey.... heard the gobble .gobble........ saw what looked like something I never saw before.....I.took off like a bullet..(I was off my leash) .... and then there was liftoff... big sucker... next time...

March 17, 2015

BernieDog made parole.. SKy says she was gettin used to sleeping on Most of the bed... She said she was looking forward to having him back home....WELCOME HOME BERNIEDOG!!!!!!!!

March 18, 2015

As I sit here on Daddogs lap... I am ever aware of my importance to him...at times he puts stuff down that isn't exactly the way I say it.. but he tries..... It seems his lap is getting smaller. is he losing weight or am I getting bigger.. I'll be nice and say.... both ... Momdog says ..without me .. He might get someting done... Daddog says he owes it to me to sit here until I make what I wish to say clear... He says how many people are blessed with such a SMART DOG.............. Momdog has enrolled me in typing class.....SLY.........The beatings will continue until morale improves.

March 19, 2015

Daddog had BACON this morning…(has it often).. Yum… He always gives me some… just not enough….. He raises his hands to show me there is no more, turns them, the whole thing……. But the Nose ..Knows…Today I sat really still….He forgot I was there..Busted… had to be 3 more Big pieces…… Got my share…Maybe it's wrong to take advantage of Old people…..NAH!

March 20, 2015

I'm a friendly Dog.. I like ofver dogs.. people .. I don't like cats, squirels, or turkeys… however I might be changing my mind about turkeys… turkeys IS fun to chase.. infact I like all birds.. snuck up on Dove today ..almost got him.. I may have to look seriously at this Duck Huntin stuff.. sometimes I sit still and watch groups of piegons when they fly over,,..Daddogs says that's what Bird Dogs do… I will have to work on the Loud noises thing.. but Hey why not?… I'll ask SKY when I see her.. maybe she can give me some…flushers…(SKY's not a pointer)….get my flush.

March 22, 2015

Here in Tahoe…made it….2 quarts of Droll but nothing else..I am trying to be a trail blazing dog.. but I'm used to my certain spots…Daddag keeps trying to tell me it's ok to Scent new places..but i've been alittle low on fluids..I did wake him up to take me out..that got me some chicken from Sizzler at 4 am…Win Win.

Shit My Dad's Dog Says - John Hugh Lewis

March 25, 2015

What a crazy couple of days…….
made it to Tahoe..,(.you know about
the drolling) … went to see MY old
friend SKY…(Bernies doing well)..
Sky wasn't that pleased to see me,, I
guess, sometimes you probably should
leave things alone and remember the
good times.. maybe she was having a
bad day.. Back at Tahoe lots to sniff
and scent…. I saw snow for the first
time.. kind of trippy,,,Momdog tried
some new pill for the trip home… no
drolling… had alittle trouble with the
change in altitude… couldn't figure
how to hold my nose and blow… well
Im home now NAP time.

March 25, 2015

Up in Tahoe .Daddog and I were
talking to a Dog breeder…(I think
she just watches)…who was giving
advice on my education..change is
something I usually resist unless
it's my idea… she did mention the
word TREAT so it can't be all that
bad…… in other related news… the
training class I was to attend has be
canceled…. Prayer works…..Seems
like everybody is having a Birthday….
just a reminder…. mines 19 oct…
save the date.

March 25, 2015

over heard…. Momdog.. sometimes
when I ask you a question you answer
me with a statement totally unrelated
to what I ask… you should wear your
heaing aids…Daddog no thanks ..I
just had a coke.

March 26, 2015

Working in the back yard… always
a hoot to see Momdog and Daddog
work together…Daddog likes to
get the roots and the whole Weed..
Momdog is more of a..Snapem off
kind of girl…neither will listen…
I like to Dig up the whole area….
Quality time.

March 30, 2015

Never a dull moment…. Daddog has some serious mental sh*t goin on ….. he seems to enjoy having more stuff to do than can be completed…. Got some FREE flafstones… spent an hour with Momdog trying to figure out where to use them… it looks like it is going to be a big project… railroad ties… gravel.. sand…. and worst of all it's to be done on one of my scentin spots …. I think I figured this out….I saw Momdog slip a speaker under Daddogs pillow.when he was asleep…. I listened very closely and heard….DO THE LIST ..DO THE LIST.. NEVER STOP… GO.. GO… GO….. I wonder if they will ask me to testify.

April 1, 2015

Daddogs brother Mark is visiting us and he has a Dog named BRUNO… BRUNO is a Manchester Terrier… I am bigger than Bruno but I don't think he knows it…. as It turns out Daddog and I share a problem.. we both have to piddle when we get excited…Daddog does a better job of controlling himself than I do.. DEPENDS… I'd like to think I will outgrow it .. but Daddog hasn't ….Bruno has Neuticals…. Momdogs says she'll explain later.

March 27, 2015

weasel dog …. I have escapted doues (2) times through the slots on the front deck…. I am after all a sevelt… seflet… slippery devil Dog… I came back ..or I wouldn't be writing this….. It's good to be the Queen …Yes I do keepem guesssin… whoes the slimDog ….LEXIGATOR!

March 29, 2015

Humans have faults… Dogs have interesting ways of expressing them-selves…. Humans make excuses.. Dogs just go on like nothing happened.. Humans fail to keep their promises…Dogs may not do what they are supposed to … but Hey what do you expect… all in all it's GOOD to be A DOG…. plese file this under Profound Do Do.

April 4, 2015

Had Bruno and I had more time together it might have been better… My size was an issue… that and I might have tried to kiss him to much… he is a hansome devil….Daddog went to chase Goof balls… He hit them with a stick and then tried to put them in a hole… then he would tske it out of the hole and hit it again… And I'm weird.?.. said he hadn't done it in 51 years.. I guess STUPID stays with you …….

April 5, 2015

Daddog got a new phone… If you ever saw 5 easy pieces.. the ordering scene..(which I haven't, being a six month old Pup Dog) It was just like that… thanks to MarkDog ..He finally got what we wanted , through to the manager of verizon..(they don't deserve caps)… Daddog has FOXFI once again..sure glad I don't have HUman problems…..Happy EASTER….. rabbits lay eggs made of chocolate. in plastic grass ….. doesn't sound healthy.

April 8, 2015

MD and DD just got back from seeing ELTON JOHN ..said. It was great..(didn't take me,, didn't even get a T shirt) On the bright side.. Markdog took care of me...we had a great time....Got away with Murder.... in VEGAS....Daddog was asked by a young lady if he would like some COMPANY...apparently they're very friendly down there...Daddog didn't understand.. and said there was only room for ONE at the machine...... It sad to hear of a young girl so desparate....I guess it was SLIM PICKINS.....I guess when you're puttin the big bucks (40 cents) you are kind of a Target...anyway it's good to have them home... I'm gonna work on the Guilt trip thing

April 12, 2015

Saw a Mamma Deer and 2 fawns (with spots) in the back yard.. Spring is here..Lots of pretty flowers to dig up..Birds to chase and did I mention Lizards…. I am told you always remember your first Lizard.. mine was a Bluebelly..almost gottem…I like to help Momdog pull weeds.(just the tops)…Daddog has many projects goin… I'm helping,, He's never to busy for Pets…. life is good.

April 15, 2015

Triped over some empties on the way downstairs…. Momdog was in SAC-ra- toe-mato for a conference last night,,,Daddog says It was all a dream and I should forget all about it… I can be bought.. not proud of it but………. he says he was just toasting the completion of Items on the list…… must have been some large items…. all those bottles, the recycle people will be happy… Hey I just got some New toys… good old Daddog… sometimes a short memory can be a good thing.

April 15, 2015

Hey you need a hole?? I'm your girl.. It is very apparent to all in this house that I pocess a great talent for landscape arrangement or rearrangement….Daddog thought our project was his idea… he is now working under the direction of Momdog (and enjoying every minute of it,) now he)we) is (are) digging up deep rooted plants.. ("could you move it over about a foot"). .. I like to work in the exact spot as Daddog…. we are really a team… dirt is flyin… business cards

April 15, 2015

Well it's now offical… Daddog says it's not April 15th until he hears…. Let me tell you how it will be.TAXMAN. it's one for you 19 for me … and The TAXMANS taken all my dough and left me in my stately home… lazin on this sunny afternoon.. Beatles and. Kinks … I try to understand him … I know he's in there.. the light is on.

April 16, 2015

Momdog just asked Daddog if he was ready to go back outside to continue THE prodject.. thought I heard a GLARE…..Daddog said of coarse HONEY…He told me in confidence… "he's just lucky she lets him sleep inside"….of coarse he was the one who found the flag stones on Craigs list..Did he think. they would install themselves…. I should have stopped at DID HE THINK … Momdog says if The prodject turns out well he might get a PILLOW….. Ah the old rewards system.

April 17, 2015

I'm the only one who saw it….Momdog was away.. just Daddog and me workin on THE project… The scene… Daddog is tearing out a deep rooted bush , in the space between the barn and the house.. .he climbs up on the wall and tries to pull out a stuborn root… the root gives way and Daddog finds himself falling toward the ground, off balance root inhand,, below , tools, woodpile, and other debries.. he has less than a second before he is scarred for life. or worst… then it happens .. he twists in midair and throws is feet forward. alining hinself with the only clear spot on the ground 4 feet below… as he desends his knees come together.. he hits the ground … STUCK IT.. a perfect landing .. the russian judge would have givin him a 10…. Momdog comes home… asked How It going? Daddog (cool as always) says Good…..Was I surprised Nah…. He's alittle sore but got right back to work… he must really want that Pillow.

a history of being a place where Dogs like to lounge. (until they're caught).. it faces the window.. just the right height.. a perfect fit for a girl Dog..(all previous Dogs have been Girls). one problem .. she has it covered with a sheet.. A Girl Dog named Genger.. apparently got all muddy and rubbed her butt on it.. … Hey I'm a clean Dog… How am I supposed to get the full experence of this Thrown with a sheet on it.. Momdog is very set in her ways… we'll see who wins…. No Sheet.

from all the pettin… Momdog is in seventh heaven.. Daddog thought it would be nice to do the dishes.. win win…in other news I got a toy with 12 squeekers… 11/2 hrs ago .. now it has 9…Wait did someone just say somethin about their BABY leavin? and there Truck havin a flat… or that someone stole the blocks from under my double wide…I didn't think we had that many dishes.

good thing we have no one living close by… I yelled.. DOCTOR PHIL come quick! (it airs some time in June)… the good news is Momdog thought of some new projects.. the really good news is Big Bern is coming to visit.. (maybe he'll bring Skydog).. he's picking up some Crap(treasure) that was givin to him (Daddog loaded it in Berns Trailer.. cause Bern was a shutin)…can't lift over 2 lbs.. happy days ahead.

April 23, 2015

Pheasant for dinner.(some of the ones Daddog shot.. no be-bees). Momdog cooked the crap out of them(crap in this case is good) Bernie didn't bring Sky with him, something about having Tail problems… got lots of Pets from Bernie ,tummy rubs too, he really knows how to treat a Girl.. Offered to let Bernie go out and go Poddy with me… said something about having special underwear… words like Depends and Always were overheard… Of coarse I have no idea what they were in reference to… He did seem to have a smile on his face most of the evening…. Maybe he'll go out with me tomorrow… as we all know going Poddy is better with a friend…….. SWORD Fight.

April 24, 2015

It seems Bern just got here and" LIKE THAT" he was gone… (tell the truth , Did you get the Usual Suspects ref?).. Bernie said he wish he'd brought-en Sky, me too.. I found out some confusing things about Bern on this trip,, Being from Michigan ,He dosen't like Basketball,, I was under the impression that that's all they did back there, the other thing would of coarse be Bowling .. and Rollin Round the Basement Floor.(.Daddog says Elton John stays with you)… And by the way ,how bout them Warriors? Well Earthday is tomorrow(Momdogs is team leader at the Creek cleanup site) Daddog HAS to work under HER direction. Heard him Practicing… "Yes mis Lewis" ,.."anything you say Mis Lewis" (and ofcoarse from ShawShank)… Piss Break.Boss?… It's good to be the Queen.

May 1, 2015

Alfie is here I think I won first prize..I do love Ofver Dogs..But Alfie is Special…He..Being a PugDog ,(he is rather low to the ground) is a challenge for me.. sometimes he dosen't seem all that thrilled to be here, but I know I will grow on him…I may have to stop weasleing my way between Sandy- Sierra and him.. he is the jealous type…. He is going to be here for awhile … so I'll have to behave (I can)… Well time to go see what he doin……….Oh Boy.

April 29, 2015

Where to begin…. Let me sum up… Prince Humperdink marries Buttercup in little less than half an Hour..the castle gates are guarded by 60 men…. what are our asessts?.. Your Brain his Strength… My steel……. and then theres always the Count. (the Six fingered man)…. talk about the perfect story.. I was hooked at Buttercup.. and Kissing Book.. Daddog made me memorize the entire movie,,… I'm not lefthanded either…Grace and Bens Gramma Lewis turned Daddog on to this story when she read it in college English.. thought he'd like it…. Duh…… Hope everyone is Well…watch out for ROUSs.

April 30, 2015

Someone needs to invent a Chew toy that can standup and take a good Chewin…My latest (a fabric Fox) lasted 5 minutes..took that long to chew its head off(only good thing about it was Colorful Feces)..There was that peice of driftwood that looked like a whale, that WAS on display in the front room.. it chewed well..Ingas Rope toy is holding up well ..but hey it's a rope… no one ever got yelled at for chewin a Rope…The latest joke around here seems to be that THEY want new furniture(that would be the Female THEY).. next thing you know I'll have to wear socks….Hey Sandy and Alfie are comin… I'm gettin to be a Big Girl, hope Alfie can hang. …. something I learned… Hot links ..get you both ways……………later.

May 2, 2015

I want ALL the attention!!!….Alfie's Mom (Sandy-Sierra) Loves me (who doesn't) She always makes such a fuss over Me.. I weasel my way betwwen Alfie and his Mom.. Aflie doesn't think it's funny. and has said so….. I mean, Why do people come here? to See Me!. Alfie has her all the time… Momdog and Daddog leave on their trip soon(I'm not supposed to know)..Fun times are a comin..I'll have many stories to tell Daddog when they get back…… I Might be able to weasel my way on the big bed with Alfie…(that's the People Bed) Momdog told Sandy-S.. it was a no-no…sounds like a good place to start……. Have a nice trip!

Shit My Dad's Dog Says - John Hugh Lewis

May 3, 2015

Well they're leavin… I've got AFLIE… I changed Sandy-Sierra's name to Sandy- SOFTY-Sierra… got her wrapped around my paw….. Don't rush me… what were their Names again? They did seem nice… got to go ….A F L I E… where are you…. ah a game of hide-in-seek…… Heaven.. I'm in Heaven… and my heart beats so that……………………..

May 3, 2015

While Daddog is away in Utah.. you are All invited to visit… Http.shitmyDadogs says.com, and read…. past posts…..(got the idea from newspoaper advice columns)…..Hey… maybe we'll all get a "T" shirt.

I grieved for almost 2 hrs when they left... Then I shifted into adapting mode.. Had Sandy-softy-Sierra trained in about an hour… It's good to be the Queen….9 days of heaven.. she even fixed me lamb chops... all was going great and then…. We're Home.. I sniffed them... (they had been around over dogs)…. I got all excited (figured it would workout better in the long run if they thought i'd missed them)... they were so happy to see me... then the big disapointment.. no present... I don't wear "T" shirts.. but come on... I am going to milk their guilt for awhile.. hope to distract them from finding out that Somethings are (as they say) Missing….Heard Sandy ask Momdog if those Dolls were old? ... got to go ..try to. do somethin extra cute (like that's hard)…. Later ..

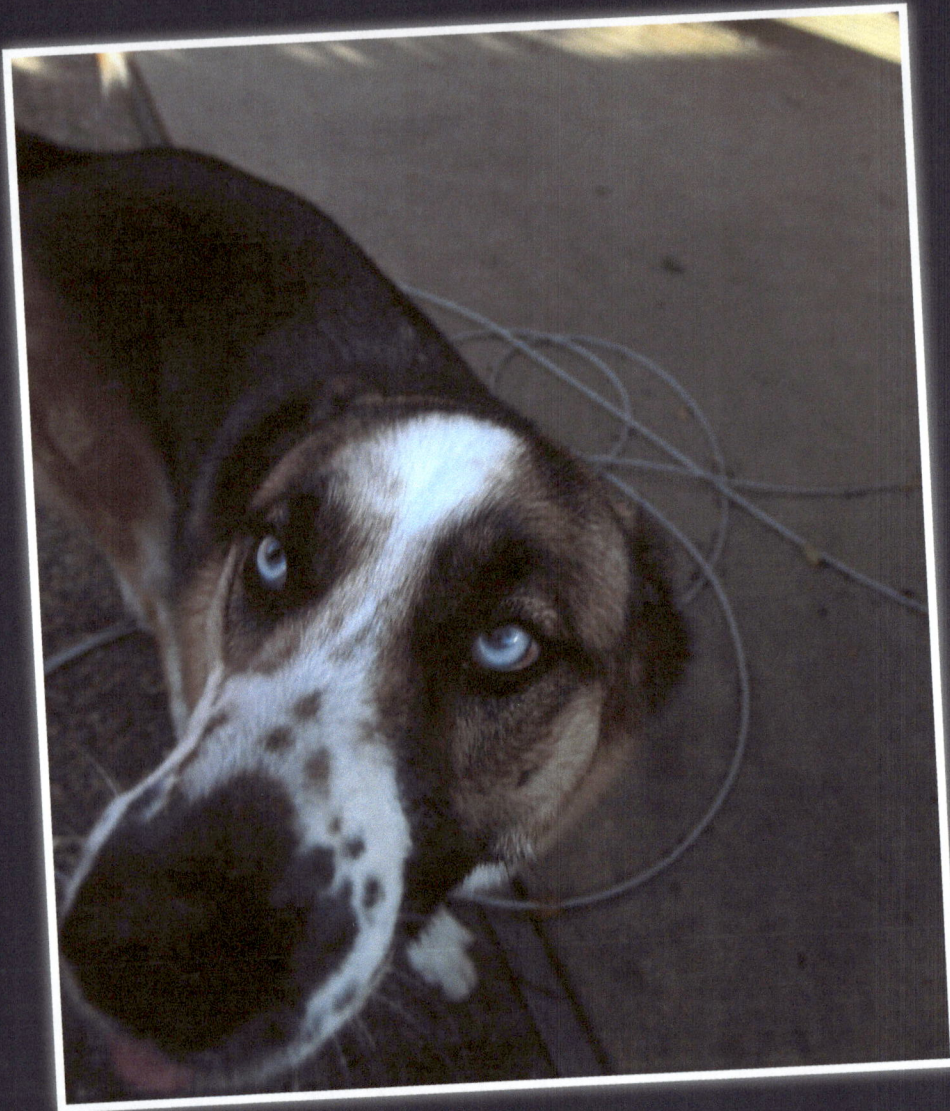

May 18, 2015

Daddog got a new Computer… Markdog came over and set it up….. It might be above his level…. the good thing is the screen size .. takes up the whole room… His posts haven't improved but his mistakes are easier to see…Hey I thought his was about Me….In other news… I'm as pretty as ever… Alfie escaped to his home in the Mountains.. I think I wore him out.. Daddog says I was pushing the Alfa Female thing.. I of coarse have no idea to what he is referring … Me being Me… My education is taking a step forward… I'm getting Tutored… more on that later… I'm thinkin typin class.

May 15, 2015

S-Softy-S feeds me very well…I have heard rumblings that this is about to change.. staements like" if she gets hungry enough she'll eat it " are being tossed around… I need a Dog Lawyer… S-softy-S is going Home… I feel THEY have created a stressful enviorment. or atleast a confusing one.. therefore I have no choice.. I am not financially able to pay so. I need to find a Lawyer who will take my case pro-BONE-O…..I'll be asking for AID so get those checkbooks ready… of coarse I hope they can change their attitude . but I need to be prepared. Maybe a SuperPac.

May 16, 2015

Finding a Dog Lawyer is not as easy as it might seem…. The Yellow pages… Yuck… use a towel next time… Google.. sounds like some sound you make at the wrong time….Newspaper… that yellow thing again…I may be Barking up the wrong tree (what does that mean anyway?) maybe things arn't so bad here afterall… I may have over reacted……Nah….I need a Dog whose bite is worse than his bark….I also need a few more Dog related sayings… I think I may have to go off leash or is it on line….Daddog would know… but he is the Defendant… it might be awhile before we hear….ALL RISE…..

May 19, 2015

My world is spinning… first a
trip to the vet ..(blood work)….
then a very nice display of
food I HAD in my stomach..
on my special back seat tarp…
I had been wondering why it
was taking longer for me to
get around… well it's called 44
lbs… got some meds for ang-Zi-
it- tee….. apparently I'm under
Stress… not getting my way will
do that to a girl.. we go back
tomorrow.. for nail clip and
something else..(it's a secret.).
once again I was fussed over by
the entire office staff.. .. I have
noticed .. Momdog does a lot
of writing in her little book…
then tears out the page and
gives it to them… they always
seem pleased… more than
Momdog.. she can be puzzling
sometimes… but maybe it's just
her way..well time for as nap.

May 20, 2015

What a morning….First to the Vet… reprieve… seems as
though I'm Hot.. fast forward to my arrival at home where
Momdog fits me with a Home made diaper..Daddog came
to my rescue.. said it was stupid..(I agreed).. now I can't go
outside without an escort…apparently Boy Dogs have very
good noses.. and Momdog says… BAD intensions…..Didn't
Ellen say something about Paid time off?… that would be
nice but I don't charge for bringing Happiness… I'm more
of the Tooth Fairy type.. I am looking forward to a lot of
quality time with the DogFolks… more on that later.

May 22, 2015

For those of you who don't have INGa in your life.. you
are missing everything… that being said… INGA posted
9 Ways to blah blah blah..a relationship … well Daddog
put that to the test… Book of Mormon.. they went to see it
last night… Daddog laughed his Ass off.. Momdog not so
much….Best thing for Momdog was they saved money by
riding B A R T…It appears ..BLISS.. depends on the sitution.

May 25, 2015

Daddog says I'm having a"Charlie Brown " moment…(sorry Amber)… My Diaper is in the dryer.. wish we had a glass door..(Daddog convinced me some would remember dryers with glass in the door, sometimes I have no clue where he gets this stuff).(most times)… Momdog picked out a plain one .(Not Daddog.. my Diaper). might have been nice to have bones on it or flowers…But in truth I don't feel much like flowers.. I feel like I've been run hard and put up wet..How long does this shit last?… and to all Daddogs critics…..B M ..(Morrison)..when you are retired everyday is a vacation da.y.

May 23, 2015

I am having this feeling that I'm looking for MisterRightDog… don't understand it,… Momdog says it will Pass.. otherwise life is good…Daddog and I watched NCAA softball playoffs.. A Girl throws a ball ..some other Girl hits the ball ..some other Girl tries to catch the ball…. I wanna play and I could SCREAM (I think that's required)..Daddog is looking into it..Daddogs event planner has I full schedule for him… SHE seems disappointed at his progress… He's a slippery Devil… Maybe it's just me but.. I don't think the idea of an event planner was his….. we are going out to pull weeds OH BOY Quality time… later.

May 24, 2015

Well I hope this HOT thing will be over soon…Momdog has me wearing a diaper.(. luckily it's a store bought one) I saw myself in a mirror.. hope we don't have any guests….. now when I have to visit the Little Girls Room(the entire Outside world) it's a Hassle…..(why did he use that word.. I don't even know what it means)..(he could have said Pain).(. Daddog takes a lot of artistic liberties) (O K artistic maybe isn't the right word either) suffice to say (Suffice?) anyway I don't like it… Moving on(darn it I shouldn't have said moving) Oh Momdog time to remove my pants… (she's got it down to a science)….. Hope your day is better than mine.

May 26, 2015

THEY came in the night and took Daddog away…Said they were worried about his mental health.. What he has been writing lately has apparently led „.."THEM" to worry about his sanity… I Put on my Big Girl pants and tried to explain that he is only writing what I dictate… THEY didn't believe me… gave him a Brain scan.. came up blank… told them!… luckily he didn't understand any of it… thought he was going on a field trip… (NOTE to self, time for some Zan-icks).

May 27, 2015

As Foghorn Leghorn.. says …".I say I say It's a Joke son"..I (LEXI) like to tell my life in the form of stories.. This.is.. MY LIFE… I'm referring to in my posts…. I had hoped .. anyone who reads this realizes that….. " Daddog" is a FICTIONAL character… made up,. not real…. well now I've gone and hurt his feelings… I have tired to make him understand the reason for his existence. (Or non-existence).. being a Dog isn't easy.. did mention I found my Pink ball.

May 27, 2015

This IS DADDOG.. JOHN HUGH LEWIS… I 'm NOT a FICTIONAL Character !!!!.….I"M A REAL BOY…. I have a Dog named Lexi…She seems to think … because I have been nice enough to help her post her thoughts … that I am not worthy of having REAL status.. thinks it's all about Her…… I always write what she says, the way she says it … and for this she calls me Fictional…She has offered to change… I have accepted.. (of coarse threatening to take picture of her in her Diaper and posting it may have inspired her) in future posts she has promised to be more respectful… and another thing… I found Her pink ball.

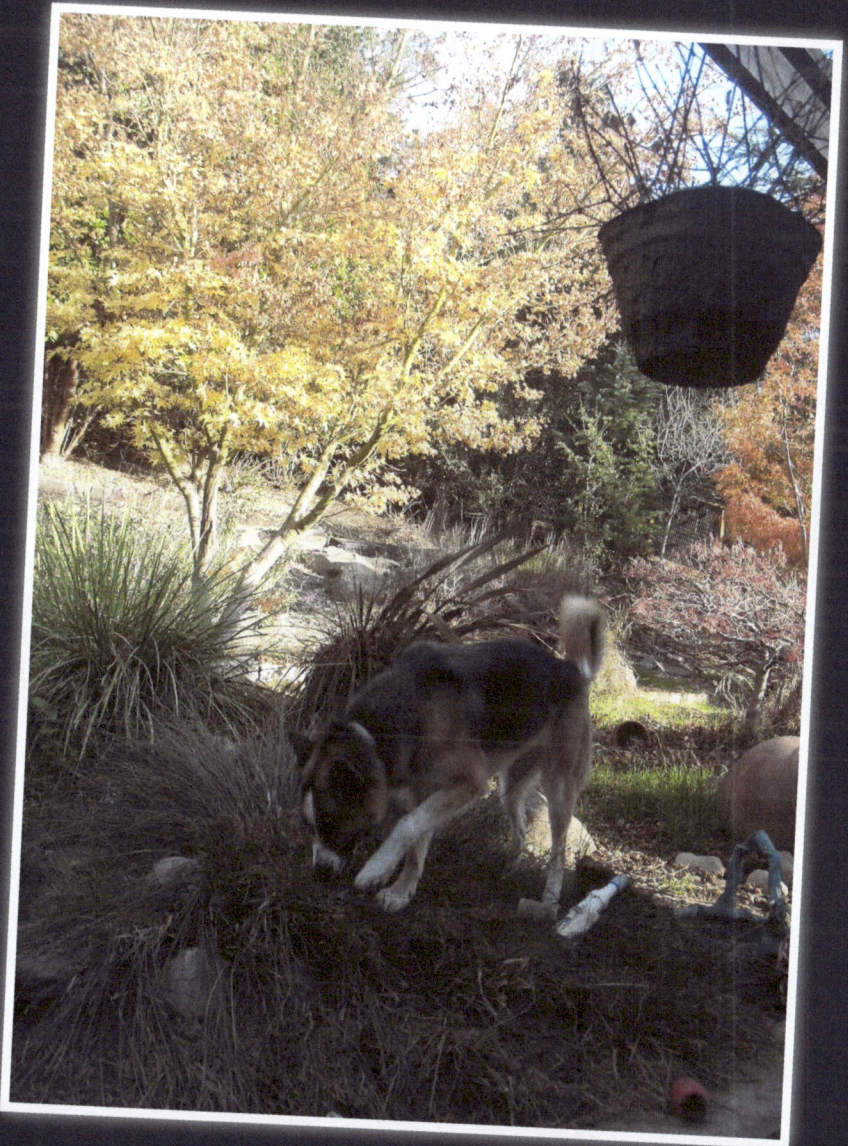

May 28, 2015

It's lonely at the Top…All is back to Normal… (if that's possible).. (someone could be happier)…Daddogs new Computer is working great thanks to MarkDog… Warriors won Yeh!… looking forward to being without this diaper…. and did I mention my new Dog run…They fenced in a big part of the backyard for me.. runnin free is what I'll be…… Momdog continues to make "food money " on E-bay…If it's not nailed down it Gone…It seems that TEETH marks cause a big drop in value.. who would have guessed… "distressed" is the term I think she uses..hope see sells something… Meat would be nice.

May 30, 2015

Heading for Tahoe…no food or water until we get there.. probably a wise move…Gonna see my old buddy Sky Dog….Scent some new places… revisit others.. some would say". same shit different day".. I say "new shit, different day"… I have always been an upbeat type of Girl…… if it isn't above Daddogs level .. maybe I can get him to post from the Cabin… Lots of Love to all the folks in my life…. LEXI-DOG-LEWIS.

May 31, 2015

Just a tease… We are Not in Tahoe.

June 1, 2015

as soon as CoreyDog calls home the"REST OF THE STORY" will be told… You will not believe it.(.Not another tease).

June 1, 2015

Just so you can sleep tonight….. the Walrus …was Paul.

June 1, 2015
S o r r y … .. . .
Daddog went TOOOOOOOO far back.

Shit My Dad's Dog Says - John Hugh Lewis

June 1, 2015

'THE OCCUPANTS GOT OUT ALIVE, THANKS TO THE FAMILY DOG'..(.ME),,,TAHOE HOUSE BURNS UP, COUPLE SAVED BY.... "QUICK THINKIN" ...."BEAUTIFUL AND MAY I SAY CHARMING FAMILY DOG'...That was the Headline in the Tahoe area after I Saved My Family..... The Scene.. Momdog In bed... Daddog Snoozin in his recliner... I'm on the couch. ... I smell something.. I Bark at Daddog to alert him .... He see flames coming in thru the back kitchen door jam......Yells. (I won;t say what).. Momdog comes into kitchen... Daddog tries to find a fire extinguisher....Momdog says"TO LATE FOR THAT.. LETS GET OUT OF HERE'...We grabbed Nothing and left..... RICH across the street called 911...The fire department came and the house was Totaled....I have been Referred to as a HERODOG..... Hey I just did what any NORMAL Dog would do... got lots of Pets.. and hugs...I tried to explain to the Firemen how hard it is to train humans and that I didn't want to start over ...A parade is being planned.. I have been asked to contribute ideas to the plans for the New house .....I feel like a Real FAMILY member...Crazy times.

June 2, 2015

I am TOUCHED by all the Good wishes and Concern.. that has been sent Our way....Thank You SOOOO much.............I have been asked to Play Myself in the Movie.

June 4, 2015

Back Home with the Dogfolks…..Being a HeroDog is tough to maintain… "And what will you do today HEROGOG??)…. I am trying to figure out how to explain even a Herodog needs some time off..Oh well….. it's like…..". What's that Girl… Jimmy's fallen down the well at the old Johnson place.?.. take us to him"…. Did anyone ever think that Jimmy shouldn't have been trespassing besides… Me…. and didn't he go off the play without Me… Sometimes I think I don't even think I know where the Johnson's. used to live… Hey Jimmy hope you're a good climber…..I need to lay in a sun beam…Nap time.

June 5, 2015

Received my "Spelling for Dogs" book in the maLe… thanks JON….(Havn't opened it yet, might be a collectors item)… In other news.. things are pretty much back to normal… the good thing is I don't have to ride in the truck to Tahoe for awhile… no news as to the cause of the fire….might have been an act of G-D-O-G…nature..There seems to be a conflict of ideas as to the type of house that will replace the old one… What is a TOZ- ma Hall.. and a Double-wide.?.. double wide what?….and do they have CROWN molding.?.(might need the old Molding team again)….. well the fire inspectors supposed to call , got to go sit by Momdog .. it will be pettin time again for sure.

June 7, 2015   I

like to talk… they call me a Wo Wo Dog…(You try and say THEIR words with a long snout.).. It's a good thing Daddog's receptive to my brain waves…. the latest thing had to do with My new room in the Ma-Hall… Pillows… velvet…. Bone dispenser.. Heated Bed….. Hey I deserve it… We could all be attending a BORING service,,, making up stories about how much we Miss them.. of coarse I would have gone to live with MARK an MINDog.. they know how to treat a Girl… So alittle space in my Honor … Is it too much to ask… Why does it always come back to Square / foot cost…How soon they forget… …sometimes WO WO has other meanings…(. A big shout out to LIsa for the Room idea).

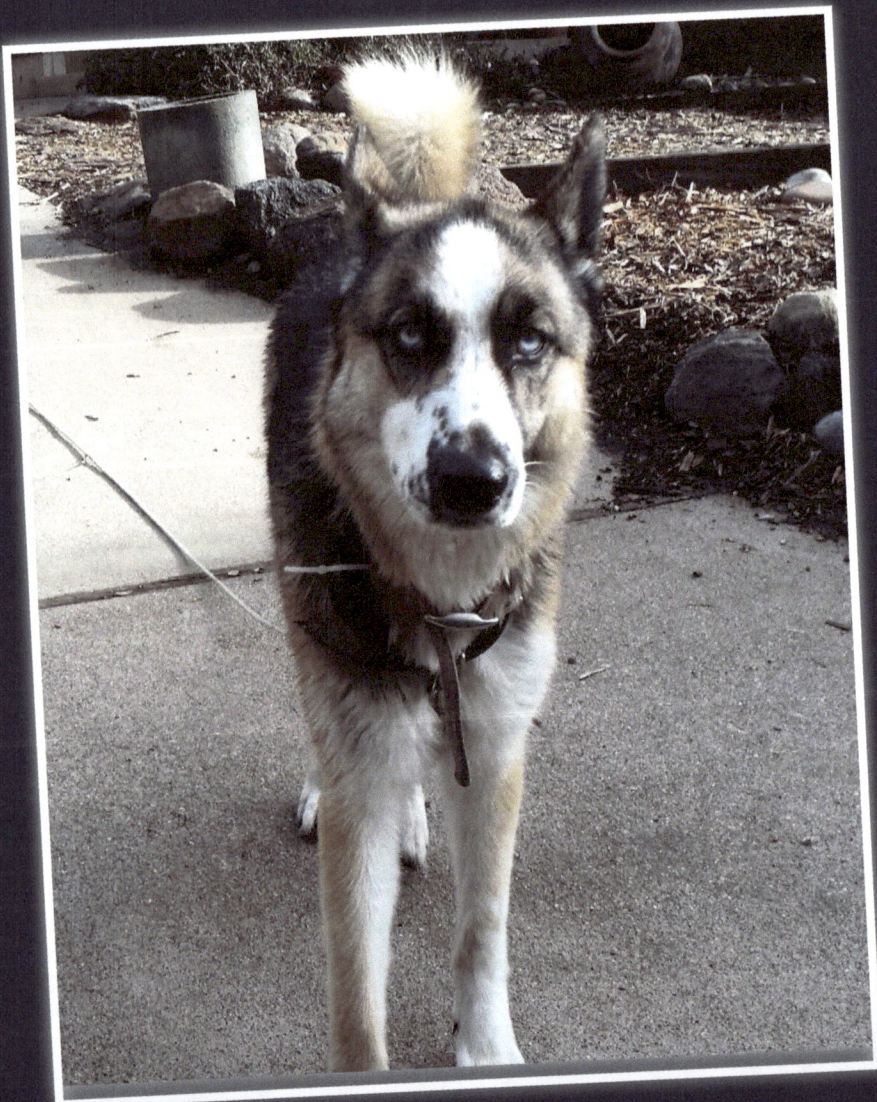

June 14, 2015

Daddog just returned from Tahoe—Sparks... Went on a mission to the Fire pit...Found his SOFT PILLOW... all was not lost...Went to stay with his good friend LIMPY-MORRISON... Fattened him up alittle... fed him Milkshakes...He is doing better -Now...Daddog might have lost some of his engineering skills... but he is such a good listener... and was able to was able to overcome distractions....(. from People who would pretend to know the answers).. everyone Had a big smile on their faces.. when he left... they waved and threw things in the air... some almost hit him... Momdog was home from the ROSE—(inside joke and none the worst for wear)... when Daddog got home... it's good to be a Family again...If anyone cares... I had quite a interesting time while he was away too... More on that later... I'm already into the..... SEE MORE.

June 15, 2015

I'm a LuckyDog.... Daddog says I have more hair on my tummy than most girls.. so my scar won't be a distraction at the beach..Yes after being a HeroDog my reward was surgery... I didn't think I was broken... well I'm Fixed now....Question....... no-one seems to have ever given a thought to how beautiful my puppies would have been...why is that?.... well I hope my Tummy hair grows back soon....What is a Beach?

June 18, 2015

I'm a Friendly Dog... the painters are here....(Momdog took some bottles back)..They don't seem to like Dogs that much... maybe a bad experience with one ,,, I am trying to let them know ..I'm more of the lickin Dog...Daddog got some Golf clubs for Fathers Day.... MarkDog and he are going to play tomorrow... chasing Balls.. I'm all for that...I'm sure my invite is coming.. Hair is growing back on my tummy area.. thought you'd like to know...later.

June 19, 2015

Ro-Bear is in town…Gave us a rendering..(that's a picture, that's more than just a picture)… he painted… our first ART- work to be displayed in the future new house… of coarse I am heroistic in it.. (Daddog assures me that is a word ,.. or should be)`.. Almost ball chasin time.. how does a Dog wear a collared shirt.?.. Warning…. (out of the Blue)…..I am reminded of a saying…." we have not been able to answer your question.. but in researching the subject.. we feel we are confused at a much higher level"….. Progress.

June 20, 2015

No Dogs allowed…… since when.. if that's what Golf is about. who needs it…Daddog says his hands are tied.. cat crap…Ball chasin is not just for humans.(No Cap" H" they don't deserve one) The retainer I have for My Dog Lawyer was a wise move.. Heads are gonna Roll… Roll..? did someone throw a Ball… gotta go

June 21, 2015

It seems everyone is upset about something…the way I problem solve is to.. piss on their shoes when they're not lookin.. gets my point across and momentarily distracts them from their rant… try it… Dog 101.

June 22, 2015

I have been asked to speak on behalf of the many speechless k-9s in my neighborhood… It is an Honor and a priviledge to be called upon to put into words what for so long has been, either ignored or misinterpreted by the Humans around us… the frustration felt by my fellow Dogs had almost reached the critical stage… Barking just wasn't working… I feel a great weight and responsibility.. , but feel I 'm up to the challenge..so that being said….Woo.,woowo.. wowowo wo, wowo-wo wo.. Wu wu WO.. I hope this clears up a few things.

June 23, 2015

My thoughts are GIN-U-WINE… from my heart…nothing ARF-A-FISH-AL…..feedback from my speech raised a few questions..it's obvious I am judged by the company I keep…such is life.

June 24, 2015

Daddog broke the news… I have been..UNFRIENDed… apparently by CAT people..I didn't discuss HAIRBALLS… ..I fully understand..and put the responsibility solely upon

June 28, 2015

They are being very nice to me…(.If they try to take me to the Vet again ..I'm biting someone)…..Usually means they're going somewhere…Even let me get up on THE BED… Something is definitely going down…And I'm not goin…I did hear Momdog talking to Sierra… Hey maybe I'm getting A visit from ALFIE…Like I always say..".Don't let the door hit you ..on your way Out"…. Hello ALFIE….. Question.. Does anyone else have a preference as to who they Travel to the Potty areas with..(other than Bernie)…I prefer Daddog… it's like we're a team….Hot and Steamy isn't `just a weather forecast.. it's an Event…… He was in

June 30, 2015

Daddog played Golf 2 days in a row…Daddog says.the area where they played" Eats balls"..sounds dangerous..hope he holds on to his.. apparently they won't let you play unless you have some.. but this is where I get confused..Daddog said there were Women golfers on the coarse… and another thing… Momdog told Daddog to just buy some more…. does one size fit all?.and is being able to purchase.balls age related.?…..maybe it is best I wasn't invited…..

July 1, 2015

Sierra…and Alfie.. how lucky can a Girldog get… They are finished with the fence..(in the back yard)…. I'll be runnin free….. Momdog packed just enough stuff that Daddog will have a little trouble carrying it.. likes to see him earn his keep… looking forward to some Quality time with Alfie… and I am pretty sure I'll be sleepin on the Big bed.. Note to self…. pretend that you're goin to miss them.. they are so insecure.. well if I can ,,I'll post.

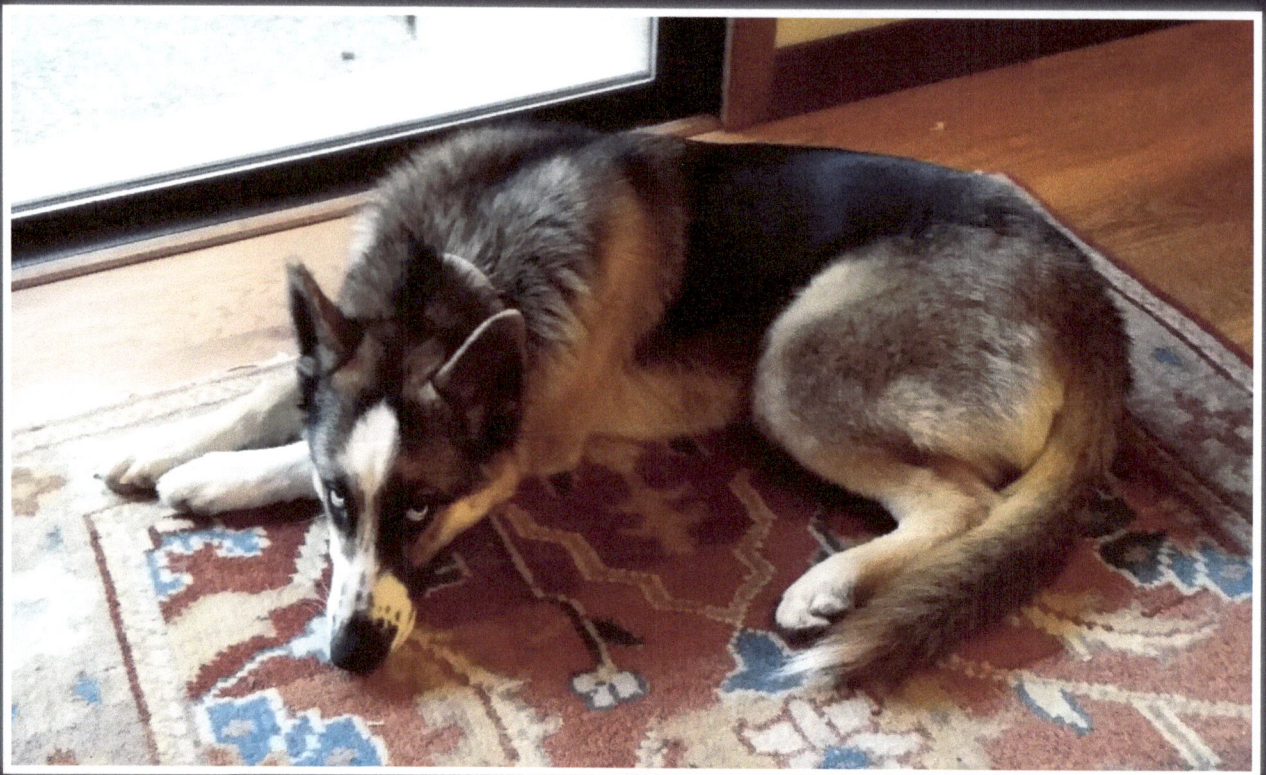

July 8, 2015   Momdog and Daddog are home… Truth be told I didn't miss them all that much.. Sierra (Sandy) treats me pretty darn good.. of coarse I went all crazified when they opened the door…Hope they never find out it was an act..That Big bed is nice sleepin..got to find a way to work" my Magic".Even used Daddogs Soft pillow..Got to figure out a way for them to Win a trip somewhere….. Daddog got some Golf clubs for Ben… went out and hit some balls..said they had a great time.. Daddog said The FAMILY visited lots of neat places.. Gettsburg.. saw a Big Bell that had a crack in it(Momdog brought FixAll but they wouldn't let her close enough to fix it) (guess hey heard about Her fixin Stonehendge) Even saw the Steps that ROCKY ran up..They had a wonderful time…They said they wish I'd been with them… Looks like we are All good liars… Sierra leaves tomorrow… looks like I'll be eatin DOG food again…Duty calls… got to look Cute… Sierra just told Momdog about some chewin I done….Hope she remembers My BLUE eyes.

July 9, 2015

I have always been a quick learner…so It was no surprise that the screen door on Mom/Daddogs sliding door got ripped to shreds…..,, When the fence got finished.. Daddog showed me how to use the stairs off their balcony. to get to the backyard..I figured what can be used to go down can be used to go up… I was banished to the backyard while they dropped off Sierra's car… I went up the stairs to see if access could be gained from the balcony off their bedroom… (Alfie was in the house).. the door was open but not the screen.. luckily I come equipped with sharpe claws..someone had thoughtfully put a metal mesh on the bottom of the screen door.. but not the top… Someone will need to be home to meet the screen repair guy… he should bring me a treat…I await their next challenge.

July 9, 2015   Looks like we might have TARGET for dinner…(That may have misled you alittle)…Early this morning Daddog appeared in the back yard with a Target.. His going"walking with Bowes" in Utah with MR Morrison and Katelyn in August He says they" Hunt Deer" ,but there was none in the Freezer when I got hear, so I get the feeling he has to take the Bow to get past the "Why are you going" that Momdog is known to say… The way it's going… I think He should call it" Chasing Arrows"… Daddog says they also Fish and ride their Quads ……… all this is done without Momdogs supervision… SCORE.

July 10, 2015

Things are lookin pretty good for us to have Deer meat(couldn't figure out how to spell Vinsion..vinson.. Venison) as long as the Deer has a big Black spot on him,…Far be it from me to start any trouble but…….. None of the Deer around here have that spot… Maybe Utah Deer do…Daddog burst two buttons… he was so please with Himself.. the way he shot those arrows….He had to wait for a Buck to finish walking in front of the target before he could shoot.. and he goes to Utah again……Why……The light is on… flickering but on.

July 11, 2015

Daddog Killed a Tree…He was playin Golf (again) and Struck a Tree numerous times..I guess he didn't know you Can't keep the wood..so far he has lost 50 balls (note" by stock in golf balls).. but in all fairness he has played nearly 4 games..Started Dog training class today…I'm the Class clown… must run in the family…I got the Sniff thing Down first time… there are alot of stuckup Dogs in the class… But I will have them thinkin my way in no time…I'm taking it with Momdog… She seems optimistic.

July 13, 2015

Momdog gives me pieces of Hotdog for treats.. I likem… It seems all I have to do is easy stuff an there is a chunk of dog comin my way.. I don't know how the other dogs are doin .. but I'm kickin but…(Mark said I shouldn't swear on Face- book) I'm on my third package of Hotdogs so I must be doin something right..I am really likin my fenced in back yard…… I'm gettin hungry so I got to go get trained…….I don't want to make waves but… these better not be made in China Hotdogs… Oh good they're Armor. "what kind of Dogs eat Armor Hotdogs?….. Sittin Dogs ..Stayin Dogs Dogs that don't jump up… Fat Dogs ..Skinny Dogs… even Dogs that give a…..(thanks again Mark)… Later.

July 13, 2015

Momdog ratted me out to Daddog.. told how I was Talking in class…Hey I had alot to say.. the oVer Dogs just weren't gettin it…..Once again I was voted prettiest…(have to make somemore room on the trophy shelf) …. it's lonely at the Top……. things got alittle uncomfortable when I was asked if Puppies were in my future….. Momdog changed the subject really fast.. I think she might be havin second thoughts about my vet visit…The Boy dog who asked was kind of cute.. ..Daddogs playin Golf again this afternoon.. Last time he got a Birdie.. buried it in a sand trap.. he was there anyway……. catch ya later.

July 14, 2015

Score one for Momdog.. She got Daddog to do something she said was on THE LIST that wasn't… you would think he would've checked.. thought he was sharper than that…. Sometimes I catch him at a Stop sign waiting for it to turn Green… So I guess I'm not that surprised…Saw him writing it on the list after the fact… He thinks nobody knows.

July 16, 2015

Maybe I'm not supposed to be surprised….Daddog is always coming up with something..Well he's. so proud of himself and his new Golf?balls… They have holes in'em… He hits them and they don't go anywhere…just like the regular Golf balls he hits except he won't loose as many… on a side note… Momdog said if he fixed the Spa.. he could use it as a water hazard… of the Two of them…Momdog is about a mile ahead…(Good thing for Daddog .. she doesn't Flaunt it) (SOOOO humble).

July 18, 2015

Life is Strange….I mean How can you be a family.. If you don't listen to each other.. care for each other .. love each other..and treat your Dog as a Princes… My Dad was an asbsent-T Dad… He Loved my Mom(atleast once) and then.. psst he was gone.. Doesn't mean if he showed up I wouldn't love him.. Stuff happens…It Makes me sad to see Humans that don't cherrish what they have…….. Just an Observation… this has nothing to do with….. so obsorbe it.

July 18, 2015

Sometimes all a Girl needs are Pets…. I know if I come in ..and get up on Daddogs lap… I'll get some…. Win ..Win… Love is that Easy…… I don't need a Treat… just Him……………(..Cut to the Superman theme)…. Can you read my Mind?….. (Eyes roll back…Tummy Rub… We are so Lucky)

July 18, 2015

Daddog had a great Game of Golf yesterday..That is until he found out was on a Frisbee Golf coarse….. He putted very well.. and even He can Drive the ball that far…..I don't think He really gets the Concept…… Momdog says Atleast it keeps him out of the Refrigerator…. He is being Banished to Sturgis. SD soon…. maybe he could read a book on Real Golf while he's there.

July 21, 2015

I feel.. I am about to be disconnected… silenced, maybe even ignored at the least Unheard… Daddog leaves for Sturgis tomorrow.. then he will go Hunting in Utah.. I will loose the Month of August…. Now is the time for Memory loss to kick in. or did it I forget..I will try and keep a journal.. but not being able to write might cause a problem… Momdogs mind is to strong to be able pick up my thoughts and my attempts a Mimery..(if that's not a word it should be).. have failed in the past…so.. I know some of my F-B-F (facebook friends(will take this hard… please keep me in your thoughts.. as you will be in Mine ……. just think…. What would LEXI do… works for me.

July 30, 2015

Heard from daddog…mom dog and bernie.are trying to retrain him..I think it's called an inter ven shun..good luck daddog…

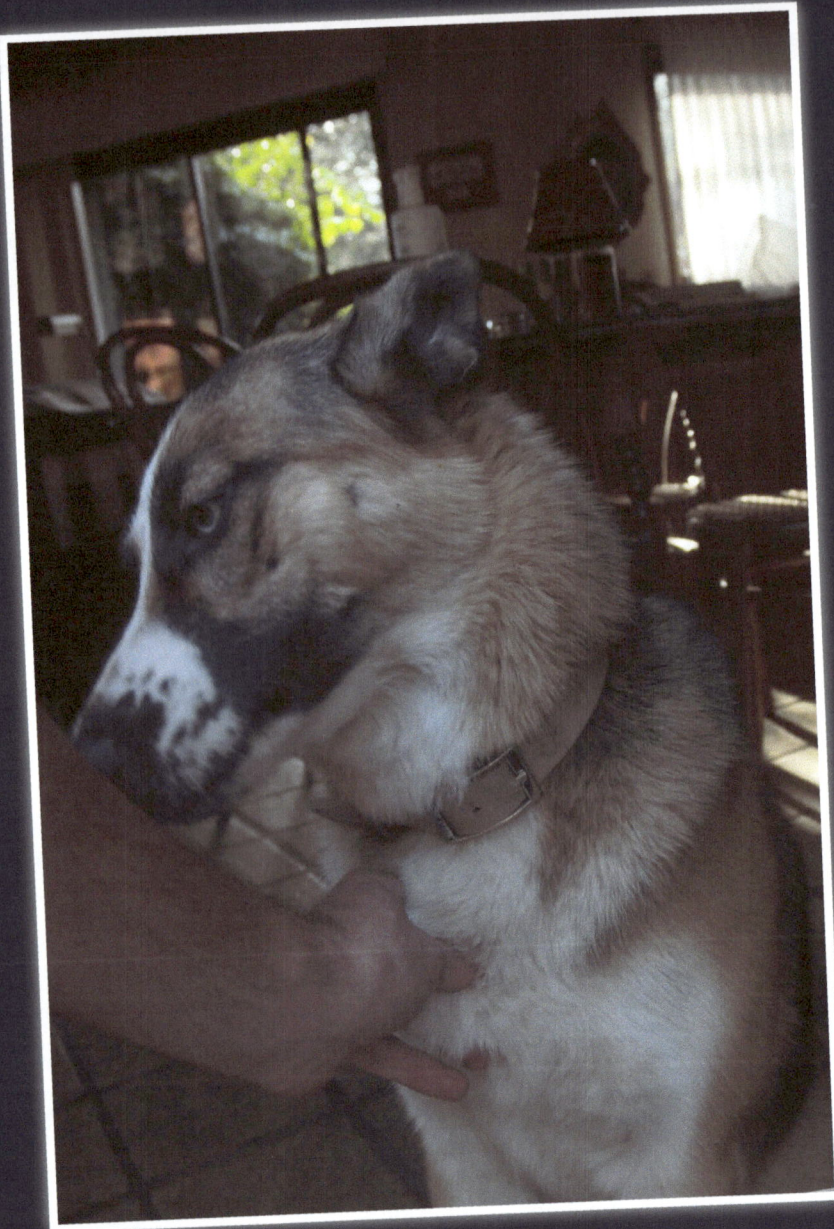

August 8, 2015

Daddog and Bernie just left Wendover. ..early bird gets the bone. It was wom ..but..this is a dog post…in other news…I chewed the fringe off the oriental carpet.. yeah the o..ne they just had cleaned..by the way oriental is politically correct. .got bored..momdog isn't happy ..my cute . needs. Work.

August 13, 2015

The movin.people have been putting daddog stuff in storage.?.. are black garbage bags ..storage..daddog is in Utah with bernie.. walking with beau's .. momdog said something about enter viewing replacements..I thought ab sten ence.made through heart grow fonder .wait I think that was supposed to be bowes…deer huntin…I confuse easily. .. You try typing with paws.

August 13, 2015

Fyi.momdog never read these posts…… daddog's secret life..told only to a trusted few..yes it is nice to be special.

August 6, 2015

Mom dogs home. Said a lot of the girls in sturgis were into arts and crafts..said there were wearing ..pasties. Hope daddog got some photos..don,t know if they were eet a bull probably better if he doesn't T fine out. Mom dog had a great time got some beads..didn.t even have to lift her shirt that high.

August 7, 2015

Sometimes daddog hits the wrong buttons. ..he and his buddy Bern are all packed up and ready to head west .two old farts. Living the dream.

August 25, 2015

Here in Tahoe with momdog.. .some fences..can't hold in a fine girl like me.. daddog is still in you ta with berniedog..so far they have killed 12 fish. Katelyn with a k caught the biggest ones. Berniedog runs a tight toy hauler. ...fortunately for daddog there is plenty of al Co haul.

Shit My Dad's Dog Says - John Hugh Lewis

September 1, 2015

Daddog called in from. well he said the wind had stopped. ..looking at my dog crystal ball. I,d say Wendover nv… said something about fishing lessons…from a hooker..I can only assume. He isn't bringing any fish home. ..of coarse. .he only has.ten bucks to spend..so I hope he is a fast learner. It will be nice to see him again…he will no doubt have many stories to tell…momdog and I have been practicing rolling our eyes..I have been told by momdog..not to ask questions. .you should see my fake dog smile. .countin the hours.

September 2, 2015

From what I here daddog..is in sparks..his therapy. .from Dr morrison..has ended..i hear there is no hope. Many nights around the campfire in uhta..and no banana. They have been friends. For forty something years but..bernie says it's like talking to a log.. the boy is stuck in his ways. I from a distance feel he is just to deep…a brilliant mind trapped in an old body..of coarse he,s all I have and from what I hear Dr morrison license may not still be in effect. .hang in there daddog.

September 5, 2015

Sittin here by Daddogs side… good to have him back… my paws were gettin cramps in them.(I'm not a typist.).He showed us pictures of the places he's been..some of them sold T shirts…. I didn't get any… never wore one.. never wanted to…He can't figure out how to share any of his photos ..so take my word for it.. some are great….when he shows them …blank looks come, eyes glass over.. people suddenly have to answer a door.. and he says the same thing…. You had to be there…Sturgis was non-stop people..over 1.3 million people. all trying to go the same place.. They parked the Morrison mobile (toyhauler) in Rapid City Had some Great rides…Momdog (aka Cycle Slu….) Did her best to maintain order.. If someone appeared to get out of line .. she threatened to send them to their room…I think all those years as a warden at a womans prison.. scared a lot of people.. Bernies wife Judy Had a great time and met many new friends.. she was really intrigued by Pasties and thongs.. (what ever those are).. Daddog said "when they left… it was like a great weight had been lifted"..(must be something to do with how a bike rides different with just one`on it.. …. more later… Pettin Time….

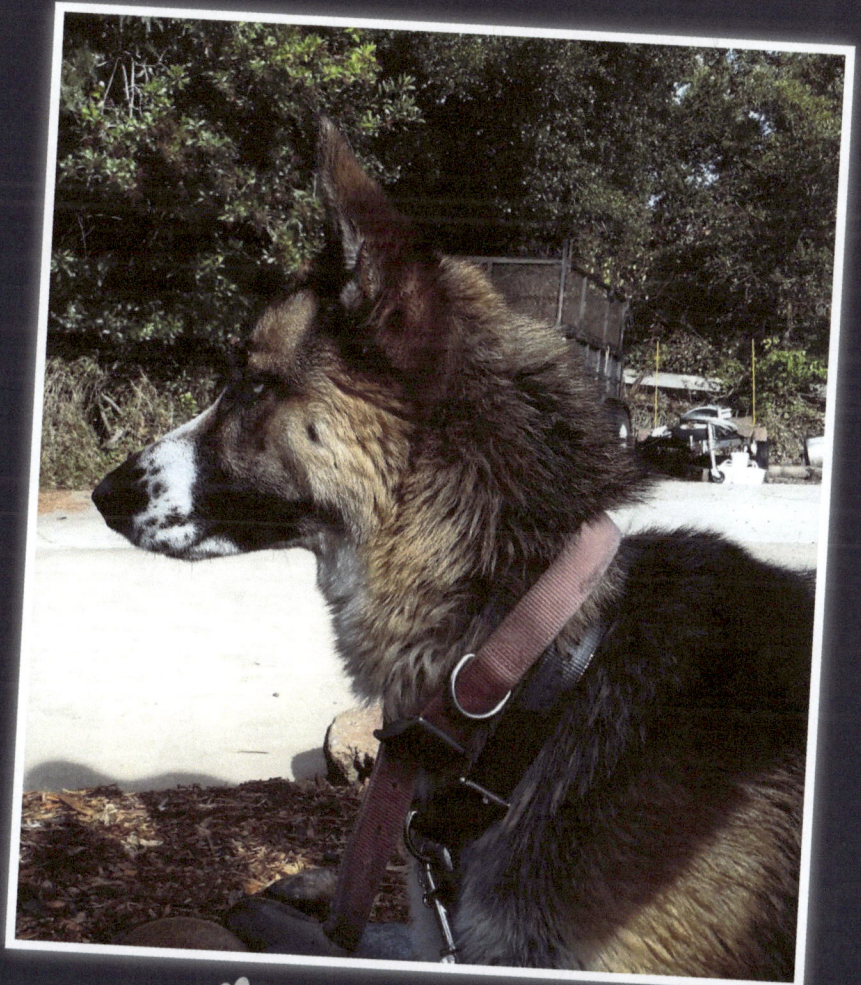

September 4, 2015 ·

Just an up date on Daddogs fishin lesson... The Hooker...(I guess that is what you call a ro- fisher woman) said "with only 10 Bucks.. He had better use a Better line"... He was reelly.... (Pun intended) Lucky to get that kind of advice so cheap...(she took the Ten)

September 6, 2015

Got a new Ball … it lights up when it rolls. ..Daddog would throw it if he wasn't doing the List…Last count ..six pages… Momdog beleives… You go away.. you pay…I on the other Paw …feel hands are for pettin…Got my report-card from Dog trainin school….got a E… cause I'm Ex cell ent.. looked like an E…. it was missing its bottom part,, Had a long talk with Momdog .. we WOOO WOOed for about 5 minutes… she didn't make much sense,, but we sounded great…. found out how to open Momdogs sewing room,,, yeah I know … I get Banished at least once a day… Yarn Balls….. heard I'm gettin a new chew-toy… a new couch… life is good.

September 7, 2015

Falling back into the old routine… you know… Look pretty ..grin a lot.. pretend to obey … Didn't take ole Daddog long… I think Momdog missed Him… she won't cop to it but… Her list is now Double spaced.. still as long but…I am having trouble relating to my blinking Ball..(and you thought you had problems) Being colorblind doesn't help, but hey some folks don't have Any Balls ,so I'll try harder …Daddog cooked dinner … Costco chicken …WIN WIN… I wonder if you can buy just the skin?

September 8, 2015

Coreydog and Vera came for dinner.. suckered Vera into being a facebook friend… I can be charming …. one more person wasting there life reading my posts… score one for the Lexieister…

September 9, 2015

I'm not a clothes girl…. (One coat, (beautiful) but just one) Right now I would really like to take it off.. of coarse some clown with a camera would take my picture.. yeh you got… it… I'm HOT. (shouldn't say it but.).. I'm a Hotdog…. I've eattin Casper Hotdogs… I now have a better understanding of their plight… Daddog ignored my request to activate the cooling machine… I licked his face while he was napping.. it worked… no more for now ..I found a register to lay on ….Be Cool.

September 9, 2015

Wow.. what a night… Daddog took out a loan and turned on the cooling machine.. I only left my register to go Out to go poddy…I owe him one… Heard on the news more to come.. bummer…Daddog said it was to Hot to Play golf..(Candyass)….He is using the Heat to get out of doing stuff.. Momdog is not fooled.. her pen flows better when it's hot…I figure with no-add-ons the List will be finished by 2020..(just a guess).. got to get back to the register ..later.

September 10, 2015

Happiness is finding a bone you buried in the couch…It helps to have Humans that think it's cute… got it made around here….. if somebody beams me up ..there's going to be trouble…. gork… clato merada nictoe.

September 12, 2015

This just in…daddog picked up his new truck today..he is still in sparks.. from what I hear..it is above his level h..e returns tomorrow. .it asks hm questions..hope it can deal with a blank stare.. Daddog is more of the go to the freezer and get the box.. type of tech wizard…berniedog told him…turn the key and point.

September 13, 2015

Daddog s new truck is really nice can't wait to throw-up in it… he seems to think I can be controlled.. there are many cracks and crevi-ieses(pronounced.. creav- vas says) the could use a little . wetness(with chunks)…… hey I'm here for Him.

September 14, 2015

The Party has been canceled…. Momdog was going away to a bowl throwing class..(yeah I know)..(They had faces on the targets.and everything() You supplied the picture).. Due to the fire in the area being 2 miles away from the place the class was to be held.. she chickened out.. thus changing Daddog and my plans for the weekend… I believe the term is… De-railed…the good news for all, is you don't have to worry where you'll put your GIFT bowl … I guess they don't beak on impact… I heard the firefighters are doing great work… maybe there is still hope.

September 16, 2015

Daddog went to Auburn… ok I'll start from the begining…Their good friend Jeannette. (of Jeannette and Arnie fame in Seattle) got so excited she decided to break her leg.. they (J&A) have many stairs at their house.. the need for a chair lift had presented it's self… Enter.. the engineering team of Arnie and Daddog… now the first thing they came up with.. would have launched Jeannette about (estimated distance) 30 feet across their street… possibly causing more Damage to the whole Body of Jeannette..(which dawned on them before construction).. The alternate plan involved Daddog going to Auburn to pick up a Factory, Osha approved lift….. Viva Alternate…. Daddog will start building boxes for the lift tomorrow..so it can be shipped…. jeannette will be saved… but I bet she would have stuck the Landing. I never met Jeannette .. I hear she's a great cook… of course anyone with that many double letters in their name has got to be … gettin better soon.

September 14, 2015

Rode in the Truck today….. drolled a little but all went well… not the new truck… old Red…. Momdog thought it would be better for Daddog to go look at a used couch.. instead of watching Football…. she usually gets her way.. besides the game he really wants to see is on Monday night… cut to the chase… the guy didn't show up.. (probably watched the game)…We shall ride again …Daddog said if Momdog fills out the proper forms ..He MIGHT give her a Ride in New truck….. He obviously didn't read the Title… the word OR is as plain as Day…(your Honor I present exhibit A)… (enjoy your new Truck Momdog)

September 17, 2015

I don't usually print retractions... I had met J&A from Seattle before..My bad..(they probably didn't make a big enough Fuss over me during their visit).. Doddog had me look at a series of photos.. Now I will know them anywhere....Hope to see them soon... Went for a ride with the Humans..(in the Jeep). Nose out the window no problems... got lots of Good Girl-s... fooled them ..saving the chucks for the new truck... the truck has Leather seats.. I think.. I'll never see them , they'll be covered with a towel,. we will see who wins.

September 18, 2015

Animals,,, Daddog has MOUSE problems.. I know I shouldn't have eaten the plastic plate off the bottom of his MOUSE... but that was months ago..now ..he changed batteries.. no blue light..He called Markdog.. no answer.. This post is only happening by the grace of Dog......when he hits enter that might be all from us... I have enjoyed my time.. telling stories with Daddogs help.. I hope it's not SAB-BO-TAGE... i wouldn't put it past Momdog... he has been very busy building a crate to transport the Chairlift.. it's done and leaves tomorrow,Daddog built it bullet proof.. it can also be used as a Homeless shelter...(I'd go back and put a coma but ..no mouse).. Daddog is hes-i-tent to stop typing... I'm going to reach over and push....P...O...S....T... .

September 18, 2015

The Mouse problem is solved.. took awhile ..Daddog went to Petco...even I knew that was the wrong place... installation required his glasses ....lucky for me , he didn't have to use his ears..He is so pleased with himself , he is taking a nap...... on a side note... Momdogs Woo Woo doesn't mean what she thinks it does... but she is trying... every Dog knows you have to pronounce the second o on the third Woo.

September 19, 2015

The scene... Back yard Lewis house...Daddog doing list items...conversation overheard...Daddog " hope there is a"HAPPY ENDING " after this" ...Momdog " you bet I'll mark stuff off".. I don't think they're on the same page...(my Bones are on Momdog.

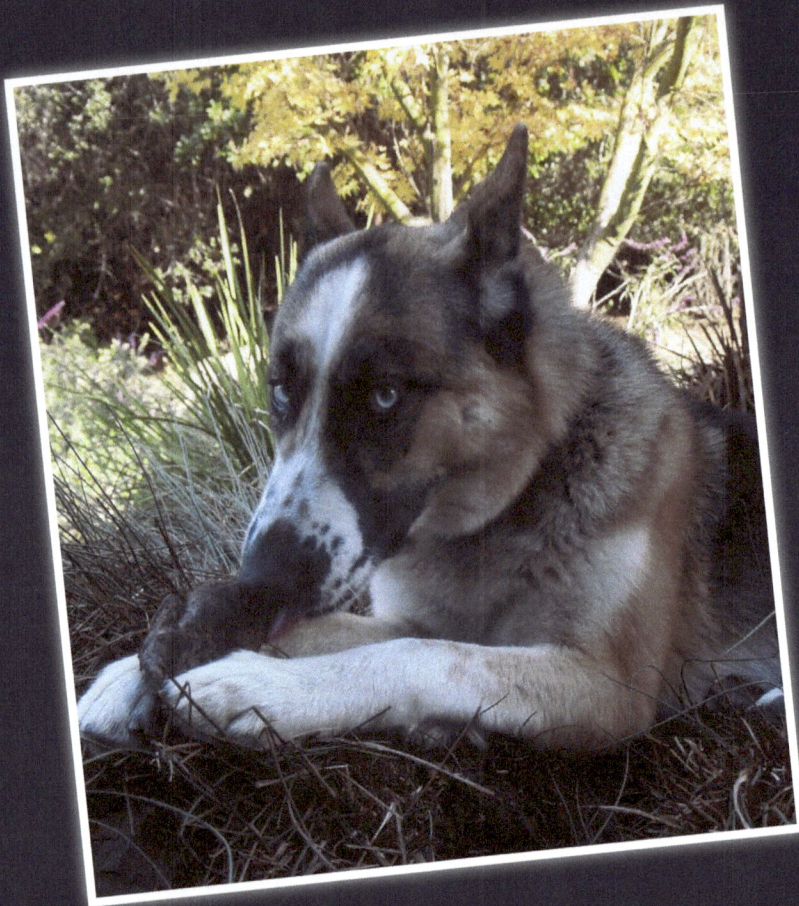

September 22, 2015

There is a saying most Dogs share.. " Wo WuWu WOOO..It means.." You're the Best.. Thanks you for having me in the family" I am a Lucky Dog, (yes still happy about the chicken skin)…However there are many mixed messages I have to deal with…case in point… The new truck… sure I have been known to drool a little when riding in vehicles..But why did they get leather if it's not to be enjoyed. BY ALL.. Cows clean up well….(not quite true.,(. I've noticed.. they don't Wipe well, but they're Cows)…..(Sorry about the visual) what could a little drool hurt…So when the big box arrived I was surprised to see a complete cover for the back seat of the truck including door sides… I believe Mr Morrison gave them the idea..He's full of them (IT).. if that's not a mixed message ..what is?. They will not be hearing Wo WuWu WOOO any time soon …

September 21, 2015

Who to complain to..My de-lim-a… Do I make my case to Daddog and risk upsetting the apple cart (I don't even know what that is) (Daddog putting words in my mouth again) BUT(Seg-way alert) I haven't had Costco chicken skin in atleast a week…Do I make some spills from my water bowl so they have to use paper towels to clean up(they always need towels)so they will go to Costco or is there another way, I could use some suggestions.

September 23, 2015

Here I sit ready to go…another day without a ride in TNT(the new Truck)….Daddog is Driving up to Middletown to deliver some cleaning supplies for the fire victims.. He talked to a Lion from that area and that is what they ask for,The lions Club Daddog is in, the Castro Valley Lion breakfast Club wanted to do something directly for the victims…Wish I could go…So sad to hear of all the displaced animals… drive careful Daddog.

September 21, 2015

Wow…it arrived minutes ago… no not the rolls of toilet paper not the paper towels…When they started unpacking the boxes ,there it was …clear container.wrapped in its own plastic bag to keep it warm… Their dinner and my Costco Chicken Skin.(of course it has to be removed from the chicken,…. my thoughts were heard….. it's 3pm I vote for an early dinner… hey i'll even sit.

September 24, 2015

Well all the waiting is paying off… WE leave for Tahoe Tomorrow in TNT….I can't see the Leather but I know it's there…. all precautions have been taken..now it's up to me to defeat them….. place your bets… A full report will be forthcoming…no bit-coins please.

September 29, 2015

I am an Easygoingirl…If I have One fault , it's that I am sooo friendly…Just got in from Morrison Meadows in Sparks NV We all had a wonderful time..Not…..Momdog and Daddog went riding on the Motorcycle.. something called Street Vibrations..I was forced to stay in a Cage,,, 30×40 ft with lots of water and shade… Why? well it seems (like I said) i'm to friendly, the Dogs we visited (in order) Srappy..Koda…Huckleberry.. and of Course SKY Dog, are kind of set in their ways.. their ages if added up would be be right at 300 yrs.. I tried to control my excitement but when you're a Young Girl Dog like me you can step on Paws very easily… Sky Pinned me down.. and said KNOCK IT OFF… a few times.. but I'm sure she will miss me.(she didn't seem all that upset when we drove away)…In other news the NT worked out very well.. not luck christening.. but that leather sure smelled nice….. one saving Grace was that everyone thought I was Strikingly Beautiful..(they didn't say so in so many words but I could tell) Well it's Nap time.. Later.

September 29, 2015

After many hours of Soul searching I have reached the following conclusion…. Soul searching Sucks….

September 30, 2015

I have often wondered .. why Momdog is so restless a night…Turns out she's writing stuff on the LIST…Good news is my new chewtoy is coming Friday…Yummy Leather furniture… I'm a Lucky GirlDog…Daddog gets to move the Old stuff out, it's going to Tahoe.. when there is a Tahoe.. Momdog calls him MuleDog…. I think He'd rather "swing on a star".

October 2, 2015

Having a great day… it just got better… the new chewtoys arrived….My mistake ..it seems THEY have adopted the new truck policy.. first thing they did was put a blanket over my spot…Momdog is very protective.. Daddog has to BE CLEAN before he is allowed to enter and sit… A clean Daddog … she wants more from him all the time.. He apparently is under the impression he owns half… Momdog said something like "read the fine print" Maybe we can lie on the floor togther.

October 3, 2015

Momdog is reGROUCHing the spa… I think that was what Daddog called it…..All I know is it's the biggest Water Bowl I've ever seen… I hear the plan is to use it to capture rain water, then boil it, then sit in it… different from a Bath because it's Outdoors… I believe the term is EX-O Bish-Shawn-ists…as BernieDog would point out… what's the point..with all those trees…Wow just got a mental picture…. Naked Lewis's…Body parts in new locations…how Sagxxxxsad.

TEMPTATION is something that just grabs hold of a Girldog and won't let go until it is satisfied... Trying to get Daddog to understand. this has me scratching my chin with both Paws... ...I'll start by saying Momdog cooks a Mean tri-tip.. which she slices on a cutting board by the Sink...Humans line up with their plates and help themselves... Now... you may remember.. how proud THEY were of my ability to stand on my hindlegs..(I know I was)... Never let a talent go to waste ...is my thinkin...In my defense why would you place a fine piece of meat close to the edge of a counter anyway? It could fall on the floor...Yeah you guessed it ...I helped myself to a small amount of Tri-tip .. small amount may be alittle mis- leading... Momdog was VERY upset... seems she had not been thru the line yet.. will they waste away to nothin.? I don't think so..They seem to think I shouldn't have done what I did..I am making the case that..I'M A DOG,,, Party planning has been put on hold.

October 4, 2015

Daddog just returned from a GAL-LA event…as arm candy for Momdog…He was told not to speak so he acted like a waiter and proceeded to get some ladies drunk.. some of them were easy.. Momdog had just enough to comment on his a good looks… the sad thing is she will have forgotten all about it by the time it would do Daddog any good … another evening in paradise…. Daddog said … there must have been "A Hundred dollars" worth of dresses at the event.. said Momdog looked Super… I had told him….(sorry had to jump up in Daddogs lap to get scraches) to focus on the one that got him there… but don't appear desparate.

October 6, 2015

I'm trying to figure out somethings… What does a Girldog ask for for her 1st birthday… And where should I register. Petco.. Pet express ?.(I don't think Dana reads my Shit anymore so I can't ask her)……How do I get Daddog to throw me a party and have him think it's his idea.. Should they rent a hall… have a huge tent…….daytime or evening event… and of course the guest list… should they limit it (and cheat pets and people out of the opportunity to celebrate with me).. should it be a Destination event…. Should there be a Theme? no, I'm the theme.. They seem to have noticed the worried look on my snout….. it's alot of stress.. I'm headed to the new couch…….Nap time.

October 8, 2015

I like to I-surp.(it's like U-surp but more on a level)..of course I have little control over alot of things… But.. know I am a force to be reckoned with when to comes to what I want….(problem is my humans treat me very good) … like right now ..I WANT A TUMMY RUB…I shall make myself available to Momdog….O Momdog.. wow you should have seen her Jump..(.always first choice when it comes to Tummy rubs)……… It's good to be the Queen.

October 11, 2015

There was some disagreement at the Lewis House… (west coast)…. A piece of meat .. fresh off the BBQ was on the counter..I felt since there was only a small uproar over the Tri-tip (see previous Posts) the Steak was " fair game"..I positioned myself to nab said steak only to get yelled at…..I did get one good lick in but only of the A_Jus (That's French… heard it on the cooking channel).. Momdog sends mixed messages… Today Momdog gave me leftover Cas-er roll…(she could have been a player in the great depression.. she makes a great Cas-er roll)… So it's O K if THEY give you stuff … but not O K if you use your talents. to obtain stuff.. Miranda had it right… "serve the Dog first"… Maybe life would be better in AZ.

October 15, 2015

So i"m laying in front of the new couch… Daddog just sittin .. not causein any trouble.. Momdog say he is distracting her by moving his fingers.. I'm thinkin Park-in- sons… nope ARTH-reye-tis…… He got up and left the area.. when Momdog is watching the news… fingers need to be still,,, it;s in the PRE -nup……He will leave for the Duck club soon …. maybe tonight.

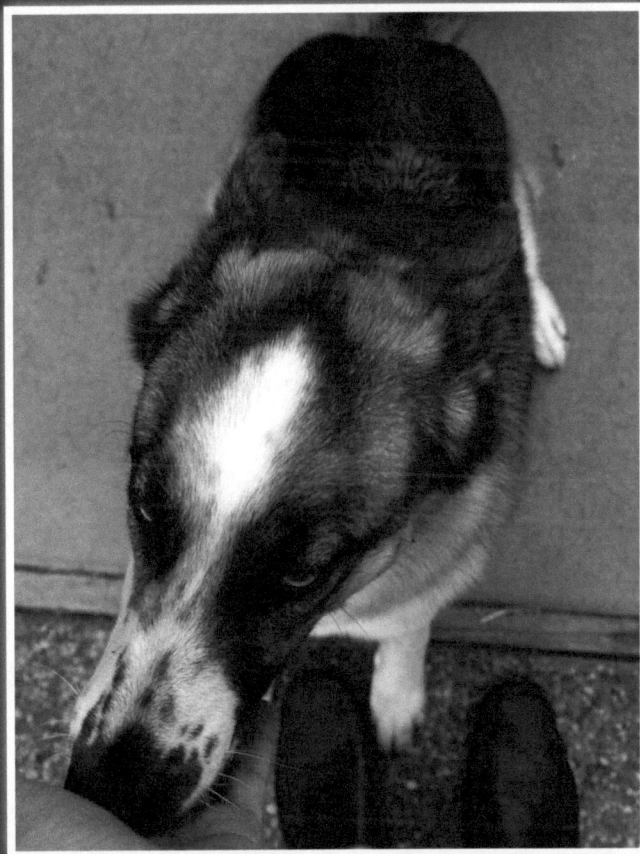

October 12, 2015

Momdog said those three little words again today…"I BEEN THINKIN".. always strikes fear into Old Daddog… it's amost as bad as…" WHAT ARE YOUR PLANS FOR TODAY/' Daddog knows there will be words to follow that he would rather not hear…The term..WE is also thrown about very loosely..as in WE need to ..or WE should….sometimes he hides… Momdog WILL find him… of course she is right there by his side helping… to say he is counting the days until DUCK season would be an understatement… I will miss watching their ways of doing BLEND.

October 18, 2015

AS the time grows near.. I find myself wondering and I must say worrying about the arrangements for my Birthday…Either My humans are very sneaky or they arn't planning anything…

I read on F B about everyone else's Birthday and how you might like to write something on their timeline.. But these —— havn't said a thing to anyone…I mean .. would it be so hard to say " the 19th is Lexi's Birthday ?..She'll be 1 human year old". apparently yes… If this is being Seven (Dog Years) … Eight is gonna suck…Hope all my Brothers and Sisters are living with NICE people…I bet if I was a HUNTIN Dog I'd atleast get a Ballon…… Less than 24hrs and their

October 21, 2015

It wasn't the best Birthday ever. (but how would I know)..Momdog served a chicken in my Honor.. very tasty. and….I Imp-pro-vised and helped myself to some hamburger that was alittle to close to the edge of the counter.. so all in all a good Birthday… Daddog said I received Birthday wishes from some special people…Hey Karen Six.. Hey Sierra… Hey Pat… Hey Lisa.. and quite a few Likes also… so nice to know you all care……. Daddogs home from the Duck club.. I havn't figured out how you shoot Ducks if you Duck.. Daddog says the best part is there is no List… did i mention I have my own space on the Their Big Bed (all of it) You knew I was going to win that one…Weaseled my way into it while Daddog was away. (..Momdogs snoring will be our little secret… Daddog knows about it ,but calls it PURRING)….. funny I don't feel older.

October 26, 2015

I did it again..Just call me SMOKEY…Momdog was hard to waken but I managed to get her attention…. I alerted her …we had a Fire in our backyard ……some landscape lights were to close to some leaves and ignited them… there was no wind so they smoldered and finally started blazing about 1-30 am . then they caught the Railroad ties they were next to on Fire. when she finally looked to see why I was so upset. the flames were over my head (3 feet high)..she raced downstairs in her Teddy(thats what Daddog calls her Oldlady house coat) grabbed the hose and put the fire out… the Firemen..(different ones) came and told her she "done good" Daddog was at the Duck club.. but atleast Momdog Had a Happy Ending. Funny they didn't make that much of a fuss over my heroics. truth be told I don't think Momdog mentioned Me to the Firemen..I guess I am EXPECTED to save them everytime .. Daddog was very pleased…. until he found out that the Fire had Sparked Many ideas of things Momdog

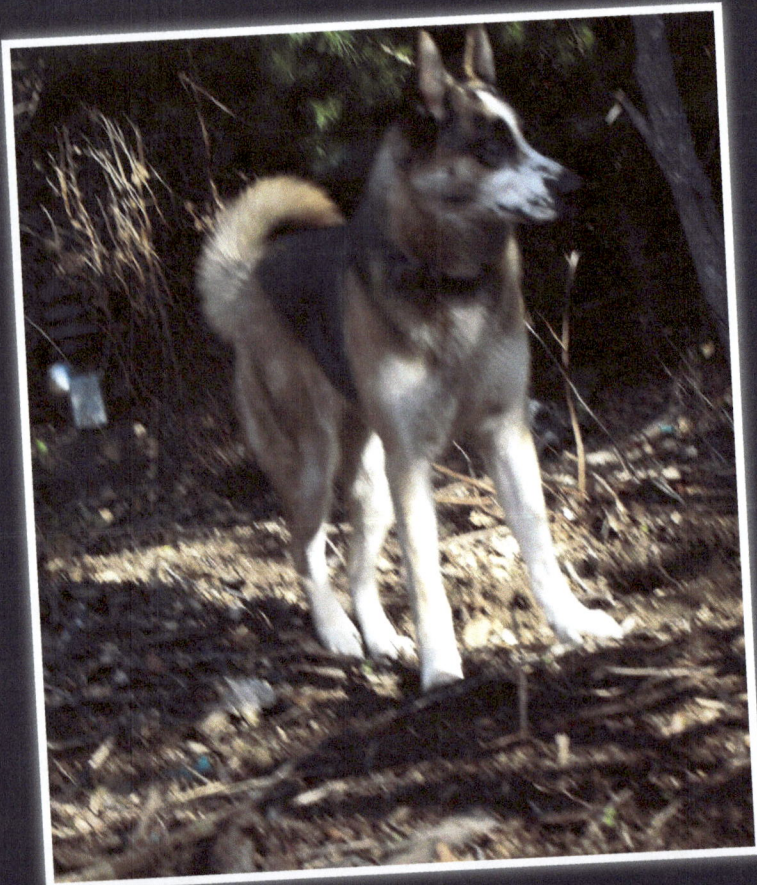

October 26, 2015

MY heart soars like an Eagle when I read the wonderful things said about me and my Fire discovering skills…All I can do is blush .. and thank all of you for the good wishes….some people were just toooooo kind in their praise… all except Bernard Morrison who suggested a Ploygraph test or mental exam to see if I was somehow to blame for the Fires.. I wish he could see my raised Paw.. that's right Morrison You're # 1… to everyone else…. I remain the Humble servant.

October 27, 2015

The GLOW of my achievements seems to have already faded… today it's quality time with Momdog in the Garage….(Daddog held prisoner by some kind of Marriage Vow)..(something about death Parting them and C S I not being involved).. she's sorting through STUFF……She is cleaning things up… translated::: Find someplace else for this…" but I don't have anyplace for it" …"You would if you straightened up your things"" You mean throw my stuff away"… "Do you want My help?" "NO"….You can't make this stuff up… Love apparently requires Sacrifice…(by others).

November 3, 2015   T

his was my first Hal-O-Ween.. It seems "you buy lots of candy and hope you get no kids to come to your door" That's the way it went here… Daddog was at the Duck club visiting Bernie… Daddog thought Bern was in Sparks but he was "takin care of STUFF" at the Duck Club…Daddog was up in Sparks(sounds like a po-10-cial fire hazzard) getting the burned up snowmobiles, when Cal told him of the location of the Bern-my-stere.. so instead of Driving Home He went by to see his Buddy.. 2 glasses of Sherry later.. Daddog decided to stay.. leaving Momdog and I with No trick-er-treaters and a big bag of Snickers..(F Y I , the Snickers are gone and I didn't get any) From what I am lead to believe.. same thing happens every year *(except for the Sherry and the Duck club, and the snowmobiles and the part about Bernie.. Daddog says it's called Tradition….I get the impression …Being Human is not a bad GIG….

October 28, 2015

Should Daddog see a There-a- PISSED…He seems to think..(I'm trying to be positive here) there are some ISSUES he can't get a handle on…He has always confused easily.. has been referred to as a dull crayon and has a blank stare often…. I'm not sure but that VOW thing..was really put to the test by the garage cleaning.. …Update… The shelves have more room on them than ever…Daddogs space looks like a war zone…(Hey he has a space?).. Now it's his turn to clean up (throw away) his stuff… I hope it goes Fast … I'm sure he'll be happier when he's done (Momdog assures him he will).. It's just getting there… wish I could set His clock forward

November 4, 2015

We have a FIRE-PLACE?.. I wondered what that was.(its free standing) ((Shouldn't it be FREE Floating?)). (((Define FREE))) But as a HERODOG I am confused…Why weren't the other FIRES in on of those ?….Don't tell anyone but it's are nice to lay in front of.. (the Fire place)….. now I'm More confused… But warm.

November 5, 2015

I'm TORN…(I didn't say that.. Daddog again putting words in my mouth) One one hand I got to accompany Mom-Daddog to the Watch place (found out.. They don't let you watch) on the other I was able to convince them I could be trusted in the back seat of the New Truck…I threw up… I love (like) to be with them and feel remorse for christening the New Truck .BUT it has been a GOAL of mine to do so..SO..I"m a Happy Dog..Win Win..? Of course I've seen the last of that Leather.

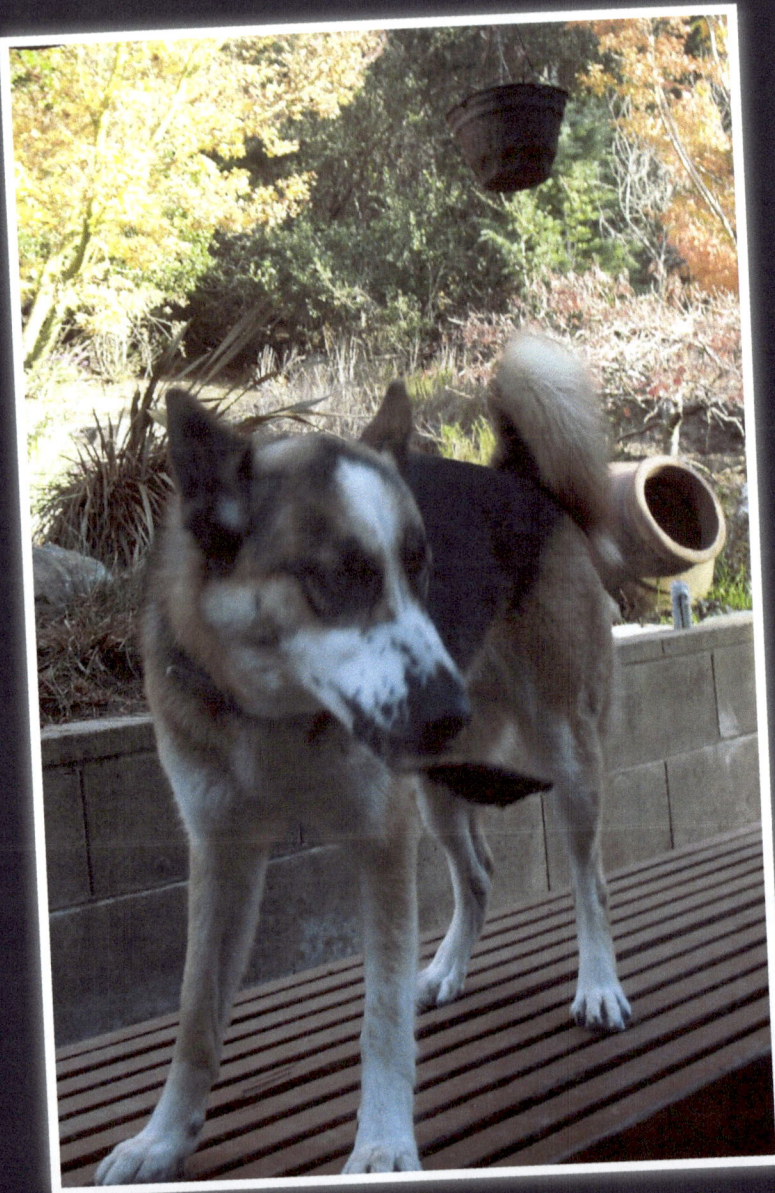

November 8, 2015

Well I have looked all over and I believe MOMDog has lost it… Her Mind… Heard her tell DADDOg we must have ATleast Two (2) DOGs………i AM the DOG of this house and I would know if I had company…. My question is "what is Shed".. If Shed is in anyway related to my ejecting my used fur.. as I travel thru My do-maine Then Maybe I can see her point…. That 's what Dogs Do… Suck it up MOMdog… (Vacuum ref)… She says she has enough Fur to make acouple of DOGs.. I say "where are you gonna get the Bones.. Jokes on her…SCORE.

November 9, 2015

I'm a Pretty Tuff Girl Dog….Most challenging situations that come across my path. are hardly noticed… so it was of some concern that early this morning , when the Sky started falling I found myself Under The Big bed…Momdog said it was because of the Thunder and Lightening… All I know is , That bed looks pretty darn good from under-neath….I wasn't Scared… I was looking for one of my Toys … Funny I've been staying close to Daddog all Morning.

November 15, 2015

I've had some great times these past few days......My old Buddy Alfie has been visiting...we don't see eye to eye on very many things...He's much shorter than me...for some strange reason..He has a calming effect on me..(yeah I didn't think that was possible either) I really like the way He has Sandy-Sierra wrapped around his Paw..Having him here is like on-the-job-training...Mom and Daddog are not learning at a very high rate..Hope Alf can stay awhile.....In other news... Daddog. just came home from the Duck club... only one of their fields has water in it.. which means .? Bernie.. had one of his sessions with Daddog ..where he uses liquid and Ice to enhance his (their) verbal skills. and tries to explain the error of His (Daddogs) ways..... from what I see ..it would be KIND to say Daddogs is a work in progress.

November 15, 2015   Me sitting waiting for Alfie to come out and play…   .

November 17, 2015

Daddog played Goof today… He and Markdog … This appears to be quite a scam.. They have a "T" time.. this requires Daddog to leave the house atleast 3 hrs prior so he can prepare himself for the main event… Then they play for 4 (5) hrs..(sorry Hun,.. got behind some really slow people)… upon arriving home.He crashes on the couch..I've got to figure.. it's just a matter of time until.. Momdog revolts..Yep… the LIST.......Daddog says that many courses require there to be a certain number of OLD folks on the course at any given time. and that it falls upon him to do his part.....He says Markdogs primary role is just to be there to call 911… and it does help Him focus if Markdog hits balls too.......Anytime Daddog has This much fun without Momdog there are usually problems...I think it's great… I get to alert Momdog that he is home and I get mega Pets....you should see how he pretends to be interested in what She has been doing all day......(The Boy is Good)..I wonder if He is a PRO-TOE-TYPE

November 18, 2015

i was tricked…. thought Alfie was just going to the store… He left… I sure enjoy his visits…. Now I'm on my own aain ..(Hey Daddog isn't there a "G" in there ?)…Now I have to eat regular Dog food… Sandy-Sierra fixes us Steak or Pork… If I knew she was leaving I would have stowed away…Hey there's a Cat in the Back yard… see ya.

November 19, 2015

When Life throws you a Bone…….Chew on it.. leave your scent…Lick it up really good…Dig a Hole and Bury it..So let it be written… so let it be done….LEXI.. Prob-blys……..(proverbs)…. (can't believe I had to explain that one)……Sorry sometimes PRO-FOUND just happens. ……..I always say.. it doesn't matter what it means.. only what it means to you…..(somebody stop this guy)

November 26, 2015

So I was waiting for Daddog to come home…. Saw the pictures of Sky and some Dog named of Buck.. Loungin at the Duck club… .. I thought it was great to see Sky retrieve that Duck.. But this Dog Buck didn't appear to be doing nothin..,,,, When Daddog got home I gave him a Good Sniff…Buck sure Smelled NICE. .. and He did look very Handsome…. My question is .When do I get to Go.Duck Huntin? ?

November 26, 2015

Well it's Thanksgiving….Planning…..Cleaning..Cooking… Baking.. Washing Dishes…Setting the table . bringing in Wood for a cozy fire… Making everything run smooth… Daddog says " Lex our job is to stay out of the way and watch football " " Says if Momdog wanted our help… She'd of ask more than10 times"…. I guess 10 is the minimum…

November 28, 2015

Heard Daddog talking to someone on the phone…Didn't catch alot of it …"when given a choice of doing something You want to do or something that SOMEONE else would like You to do …. you are not really being given a CHOICE" " You are being Tested" THEIR hope is you will do the RIGHT thing"…..When you hear these words " Do what you want" always do the opposite….Happy Wife Happy Life……I can't believe Daddog sometimes… He could have said .."Do as I say .not as I do " He always in the Dog house for failing these tests…I think the word WISE-MAN is an oxymoron.

November 29, 2015   Trying to get momdog to move over - Loving the big bed.

November 29, 2015

You tell me if I was IN the wrong…Momdog brought home a large soup type Beef bone for ME..to chew up…Did I say Large..yes I did…Not the kind of bone ,that can be chewed up in one laying..it IS a very tasty bone..Having picked up some of Momdogs frugal ways. I decided to bury it..IN THE NEW COUCH.. all was fine until Momdog found it….and I'm a BAD DOG ?

December 5, 2015

Always something to learn. The scene… The dark of night.. (not dark and Stormy)..I asked Daddog to let me out to Pee.. He's so nice to me… I go out and He waits for me to return…He says He knew something was wrong when He heard me bark (i'm a Quiet Girl)… Well there I was taking in the cool night air when….I hear a sound off to my right.. I turn an see a Big Cat Like creature….(Clue)… I don't Care for Cats.. I yell at IT to vacate the property..Darn thing lifts it BIG TAIL and Shoots what ended up being a liquid worst than Pee right in my face… Daddog says it was a Skunk.. and that's not the worst part.. Had to have a.BAFFE.. Daddog says IT must have been ROCKY's Skunk.(Rocky used to get SKUNKED ALOT)… I told Daddog .."This means WAR" He said I should choose my battles..Dadddog says I SMELL better.. but the HUGS have been fewer…… some lessons should be learned from OTHERS……

December 7, 2015

Didn't sleep that well last night....and when I don't sleep... NO-body sleeps...Maybe it was that I was feeling guilty for chewin up one of Daddogs huntin hats.. Nah...Maybe I was feelin bad about givin Momdog Poison Oak.... No that wasn't it either..(although not my finest hour.)....Was it because of all the troubles in the world...(Hadn't noticed..I'm a DOG).... Momdog said it was because I didn't have a Nap...(I never miss Nap-time).. I did get a headache from hearing Daddog yell something about the WE Won....(His friend Rick always tells him."You didn't Play")..Could have gotten BAD-TREATS ..another Oxy -Moron.... (give it a rest Daddog)... Hope I figure it out before tonight... Might be sleepin in the Garage.. Humans are funny that way.

December 8, 2015

An up-date (for everyone-anyone) My truck-sick days are less frequent but still a problem..Momdog got some special covers for truck and car, they have areas of less resistance.. I seem attracted to....Daddog is very forgiving.. (can you feel his influence..always makes himself look good in MY POSTS)... In other news everyone slept Well last night.. Havn't wanted to go into the backyard much... I think THAT creature is waiting for me..Being sprayed isn't any fun..I'm trying not to be a Scared-dee-DOG....That thing should be Scared of me... I'll work through it

December 9, 2015

Crisis was avert -ted yesterday… N…o not a terrorist threat.. not anything that endangered the free world,,. but something that has caused great frustration in the Lewis House hold.. fortunately the answer was found by Daddogs No.2 son Markdog… Who… (if he keeps this kind of focus up may move up to the No. 1 1/2 spot).. Who (once again.).. went above and beyond to solve a major concern that had been plaguing Daddog for some time.. and it was as simple as 3 and 4..(no I didn't say 1& 2).You might say he IRONED it out…O K enough suspense Markdog found Daddog a replacement for Daddogs 3 & 4 Irons.. which Daddog had retrieved from an Old golf-bag in the garage.. the 2 Irons alone had caused many problems for Daddog on every coarse he had played… today I witnessed Daddog using the Newly purchased Irons .. hittin Faux golf-balls into his practice net (doesn't everyone have one of these).. Upon Momdogs arrivial home .. the question arouse as to the COST of said new Irons..Daddog automatically went on the defensive.. after-all Cost is not a concern when IMPROVEMENT is the Goal…. but after much Himin and Hawin he confessed, Markdog had found the clubs for 398.. Momdog was agassed until Daddog told her it was 398 cents from Play-it-again sports (he loves messing with her) Daddog and Markdog had chicken wings to celebrate…. Now we'll see if he can hit real balls……. I'll keep you informed.

The End ... For now.

To continue the adventure, follow Lexi at
www.ShitMyDadsDogSays.com